Tony Harrison was born in Leeds in 1937. He has published several books of poetry, including *The Loiners*, which won the Geoffrey Faber Memorial Prize in 1972, and *Continuous*. He has written much dramatic verse in the form of libretti for the Metropolitan Opera, New York, and for collaborations with several leading modern composers, including *Yan Tan Tethera* (with Harrison Birtwistle), which was shown on Channel 4 and had its theatre première on the South Bank in 1986. He has written verse texts for the National Theatre, including *The Misanthrope* (1973), *Phaedra Britannica* (1975), *Bow Down* (1977), *The Oresteia* (1981), which was performed at the ancient Greek theatre of Epidaurus and was awarded the European Poetry Translation Prize in 1983, and the much-acclaimed *The Mysteries* (1985). Both *The Oresteia* and *The Mysteries* were broadcast on Channel 4. He is the author of *Theatre Works 1973–1985* (1985, Penguin 1986) and two long poems *v.* and *The Fire-Gap*, both published in 1985.

Tony Harrison

Selected Poems

Second Edition

Penguin Books

PENGUIN BOOKS

Published by the Penguin Group
27 Wrights Lane, London w8 5tz, England
Viking Penguin Inc., 40 West 23rd Street, New York, New York 10010, USA
Penguin Books Australia Ltd, Ringwood, Victoria, Australia
Penguin Books Canada Ltd, 2801 John Street, Markham, Ontario, Canada l3r 1b4
Penguin Books (NZ) Ltd, 182–190 Wairau Road, Auckland 10, New Zealand

Penguin Books Ltd, Registered Offices: Harmondsworth, Middlesex, England

This selection first published 1984
Published simultaneously by Viking
Second edition 1987
10 9 8 7 6 5 4 3

Copyright © Tony Harrison, 1984, 1987
All rights reserved

The acknowledgements on pp. 11–12 constitute
an extension of this copyright page

Made and printed in Great Britain by
Richard Clay Ltd, Bungay, Suffolk
Set in Monophoto Ehrhardt

for Teresa

'. . . son io il poeta,
essa la poesia.'

Contents

Acknowledgements   11

Thomas Campey and the Copernican System   13
Ginger's Friday   15
The Pocket Wars of Peanuts Joe   16
Allotments   18
Doodlebugs   20
The White Queen
  1. Satyrae   21
  2. The Railroad Heroides   27
  3. Travesties   29
  4. Manica   31
  5. *from* The Zeg-Zeg Postcards   35
The Heart of Darkness   38
The Songs of the PWD Man I, II   41
The Death of the PWD Man   45
Schwiegermutterlieder   50
The Curtain Catullus   52
The Bedbug   54
Curtain Sonnets
  1. Guava Libre   55
  2. The Viewless Wings   56
  3. Summer Garden   57
  4. The People's Palace   58
  5. Prague Spring   59
The Nuptial Torches   60
Newcastle is Peru   63
Durham   69
Ghosts: Some Words Before Breakfast   72

Palladas: Poems   77

Sentences
  1. Brazil   95
  2. Fonte Luminosa   96
  3. Isla de la Juventud   98
  4. On the Spot   99
Voortrekker   101

The Bonebard Ballads
  1. The Ballad of Babelabour   102
  2. The Ballad of the Geldshark   104
  3. 'Flying Down to Rio': A Ballad of Beverly Hills   105
Social Mobility   107

from The School of Eloquence

ONE

On Not Being Milton   112
The Rhubarbarians I, II   113
Study   115
Me Tarzan   116
Wordlists I, II, III   117
Classics Society   120
National Trust   121
Them & [uz] I, II   122
Working   124
Cremation   125

TWO

Book Ends I, II   126
Confessional Poetry   128
Next Door I, II, III, IV   129
Long Distance I, II   133
Flood   135
The Queen's English   136
Aqua Mortis   137
Grey Matter   138
An Old Score   139
Still   140
A Good Read   141
Isolation   142
Continuous   143
Clearing I, II   144
Illuminations I, II, III   146
Turns   149
Punchline   150
Currants I, II   151
Breaking the Chain   153
Changing at York   154
Marked With D.   155

A Piece of Cake   156
The Morning After I, II   157
Old Soldiers   159
A Close One   160
'Testing the Reality'   161
The Effort   162
Bye-Byes   163
Blocks   164
Jumper   165
Bringing Up   166
Timer   167
Fire-eater   168
Pain-Killers I, II   169
Background Material   171

THREE

Self Justification   172
Divisions I, II   173
History Classes   175
Stately Home   176
Lines to my Grandfathers I, II   177
The Earthen Lot   179
Remains   180
Dichtung und Wahrheit   181
Art & Extinction
  1. The Birds of America   182
    i. John James Audubon (1785–1851) 182
    ii. Weeki Wachee   183
    iii. Standards   184
  2. Loving Memory   185
  3. Looking Up   186
  4. Killing Time   187
  5. Dark Times   188
  6. t'Ark   189

Facing North   190
A Kumquat for John Keats   192
Skywriting   196
The Call of Nature   199
Giving Thanks   200
Oh, Moon of Mahagonny!   201
The Red Lights of Plenty   203

The Heartless Art   206
The Lords of Life   209
The Fire-Gap   214
Following Pine   220
Cypress & Cedar   230
v.   235

Acknowledgements

Thanks are due to the following publishers and periodicals for permission to reprint poems in this book:

London Magazine Editions – for 'Thomas Campey and the Copernican System', 'Ginger's Friday', 'The Pocket Wars of Peanuts Joe', 'Allotments', 'The White Queen', 'The Heart of Darkness', 'The Songs of the PWD Man', 'The Death of the PWD Man', 'Schwiegermutterlieder', 'The Curtain Catullus', 'The Bedbug', 'The Nuptial Torches', 'Newcastle is Peru' and 'Ghosts: Some Words Before Breakfast' from *The Loiners*, 1970

Anvil Press Poetry – for the complete text of *Palladas: Poems*, 1975 and for 'The Morning After I, II', 'Bye-Byes', 'Testing the Reality', 'The Effort', 'Jumper' and 'Changing at York' from *Ten Sonnets from the School of Eloquence*, 1987

Rex Collings Ltd – for 'Doodlebugs', 'Curtain Sonnets', 'Durham', 'Sentences', 'Voortrekker', 'The Bonebard Ballads', 'Social Mobility' and 'History Classes' from *The School of Eloquence*, 1978; and for 'On Not Being Milton', 'The Rhubarbarians I, II', 'Study', 'Me Tarzan', 'Wordlists I, II, III', 'Classics Society', 'National Trust', 'Them & [uz] I, II', 'Working', 'Cremation', 'Book Ends I, II', 'Next Door I, II, III, IV', 'Long Distance I, II', 'Continuous', 'Clearing I, II', 'Illuminations I, II, III', 'Turns', 'Punchline', 'Marked With D.', 'A Close One', 'Blocks', 'Bringing Up', 'Timer', 'Fireeater', 'Background Material', 'Self Justification', 'Divisions I, II', 'Lines to my Grandfathers I, II', 'The Earthen Lot', 'Dichtung und Wahrheit', 'The Birds of America: (i) John James Audubon (1785–1851), (iii) Standards', 'Loving Memory', 'Looking Up', 'Killing Time' and 't'Ark' from *Continuous*, 1981

Bloodaxe Books Ltd – for 'A Kumquat for John Keats' which was published as a pamphlet in 1981; for 'Oh, Moon of Mahagonny!' from *U.S. Martial*, 1981; 'The Fire-Gap', 1985 and 'v.', 1985

Encounter – for 'Confessional Poetry', 'Flood', 'The Queen's English', 'Aqua Mortis' and 'Remains'

The Times Literary Supplement – for 'Grey Matter', 'An Old Score', 'Still', 'A Good Read', 'Facing North', 'Giving Thanks', 'The Red Lights of Plenty', 'The Fire-Gap', 'The Heartless Art' and 'Cypress & Cedar'

Observer – for 'Isolation', 'Pain-Killers I, II', 'Breaking the Chain' and 'Old Soldiers'

London Review of Books for 'v.'

Poetry Books Society Supplement – for 'Currants I, II'

Quarto – for 'A Piece of Cake'

Stand – for 'Stately Home'

Firebird 3 (Penguin Books, 1984) – for 'Birds of America: (ii) Weeki Wachee' and 'The Lords of Life'

PN Review – for 'Dark Times' and 'Skywriting'

New Statesman – for 'The Call of Nature'

Iron – for 'Divisions I'

Thomas Campey and the Copernican System

The other day all thirty shillings' worth
Of painfully collected waste was blown
Off the heavy handcart high above the earth,
And scattered paper whirled around the town.

The earth turns round to face the sun in March,
He said, resigned, *it's bound to cause a breeze*.
Familiar last straws. His back's strained arch
Questioned the stiff balance of his knees.

Thomas Campey, who, in each demolished home,
Cherished a Gibbon with a gilt-worked spine,
Spengler and Mommsen, and a huge, black tome
With Latin titles for his own decline:

Tabes dorsalis; veins like flex, like fused
And knotted flex, with a cart on the cobbled road,
He drags for life old clothing, used
Lectern bibles and cracked Copeland Spode,

Marie Corelli, Ouida and Hall Caine
And texts from Patience Strong in tortoise frames.
And every pound of this dead weight is pain
To Thomas Campey (Books) who often dreams

Of angels in white crinolines all dressed
To kill, of God as Queen Victoria who grabs
Him by the scruff and shoves his body pressed
Quite straight again under St Anne's slabs.

And round Victoria Regina the Most High
Swathed in luminous smokes like factories,
These angels serried in a dark, Leeds sky
Chanting *Angina –a, Angina Pectoris*.

Keen winter is the worst time for his back,
Squeezed lungs and damaged heart; just one
More sharp turn of the earth, those knees will crack
And he will turn his warped spine on the sun.

Leeds! Offer thanks to that Imperial Host,
Squat on its thrones of Ormus and of Ind,
For bringing Thomas from his world of dust
To dust, and leisure of the simplest kind.

Ginger's Friday

Strawberries being bubbled in great vats
At *Sunny Sunglow*'s wafted down the aisle.
He heard the scuffled vestments through the slats
And could not see but felt a kindly smile.
Grateful, anonymous, he catalogued his sin,
The stolen postcards and allotment peas;
How from his attic bedroom he'd looked in
On Mrs Daley, all-bare on her knees,
Before her husband straddled in his shirt,
And how he'd been worked up by what he saw;
How he'd fiddled with his thing until it hurt
And spurted sticky stuff onto the floor.
And last his dad's mauve packet of balloons
He'd blown up, filled with water, and tried on;
And then relief. The hidden priest intones:
Remember me to Mrs Kelly, John.

He loitered, playing taws until the dark
Of bad men with their luring spice and shell-
shocked feelers edged onto the empty park,
And everything that moved was off to tell.
His gaslamp shadows clutched him as he ran
Shouting his *Aves. Paternosters* stuck
At *peccata*, and the devil with his huge jam pan
Would change his boiled-up body back to muck.
And no Hail Marys saved him from that Hell
Where Daley's and his father's broad, black belts
Cracked in the kitchen, and, blubbering, he smelt
That burning rubber and burnt bacon smell.

The Pocket Wars of Peanuts Joe

'Poor old sport,
he got caught
right in the mangle.'

The -*nuts* bit really -*nis*. They didn't guess
Till after he was dead, then his sad name
Was bandied as a dirty backstreet Hess,
A masturbator they made bear the blame
For all daubed swastikas, all filthy scrawl
In Gents *and* Ladies, YANK GO HOME
Scratched with a chisel on the churchyard wall;
The vicar's bogey against wankers' doom.

We knew those adult rumours just weren't true.
We did it often but our minds stayed strong.
Our palms weren't cold and tacky and they never grew
Those tell-tale matted tangles like King Kong.
We knew that what was complicated joy
In coupled love, and for lonely men relief,
For Joe was fluted rifling, no kid's toy
He fired and loaded in his handkerchief.
Some said that it was shell-shock. They were wrong.
His only service was to sing *The Boers
Have Got My Daddy* and *The Veteran's Song*
And window-gazing in the Surplus Stores.
In allotment dugouts, nervous of attack,
Ambushing love-shadows in the park,
His wishes shrapnel, Joe's ack-ack *ejac-
ulatio* shot through the dark
Strewn, churned up trenches in his head.
Our comes were colourless but Joe's froze,
In wooshed cascadoes of ebullient blood-red,
Each flushed, bare woman to a glairy pose.

'VD Day' jellies, trestle tables, cheers
For Ruskis, Yanks and Desert Rats with guns
And braces dangling, drunk; heaped souvenirs:
Swastikas, Jap tin hats and Rising Suns.
The Victory bonfire settled as white ash.
The accordion stopped Tipperarying.
It was something solemn made Joe flash
His mitred bishop as they played *The King*.
Happy and Glorious . . . faded away. *Swine!*
The disabled veteran with the medals cried.
The ARP tobacconist rang 999.
The Desert Rats stood guard on either side.
Two coppers came, half-Nelsoned, frog-
marched poor Penis off to a cold clink.
He goosestepped backwards and crowds saw the cock
That could gush Hiroshimas start to shrink.

A sergeant found him gutted like a fish
On army issue blades, the gormless one,
No good for cannon fodder. His last wish
Bequeathed his gonads to the Pentagon.

Allotments

Choked, reverted *Dig for Victory* plots
Helped put more bastards into Waif Home cots
Than anywhere, but long before my teens
The Veterans got them for their bowling greens.
In Leeds it was never *Who* or *When* but *Where*.
The bridges of the slimy River Aire,
Where Jabez Tunnicliffe, for love of God,
Founded the *Band of Hope* in eighteen odd,
The cold canal that ran to Liverpool,
Made hot trickles in the knickers cool
As soon as flow. The graveyards of Leeds 2
Were hardly love-nests but they had to do –
Through clammy mackintosh and winter vest
And rumpled jumper for a touch of breast.
Stroked nylon crackled over groin and bum
Like granny's wireless stuck on Hilversum.
And after love we'd find some epitaph
Embossed backwards on your arse and laugh.
And young, we cuddled by the abattoir,
Faffing with fastenings, never getting far.
Through sooty shutters the odd glimpsed spark
From hooves on concrete stalls scratched at the dark
And glittered in green eyes. Cowclap smacked
Onto the pavings where the beasts were packed.
And offal furnaces with clouds of stench
Choked other couples off the lychgate bench.

The Pole who caught us at it once had smelt
Far worse at Auschwitz and at Buchenwald,
He said, and, pointing to the chimneys, *Meat!*
Zat is vere zey murder vat you eat.
And jogging beside us, *As Man devours*
Ze flesh of animals, so vorms devour ours.

It's like your anthem, Ilkla Moor Baht 'at.
Nearly midnight and that gabbling, foreign nut
Had stalled my coming, spoilt my appetite
For supper, and gave me a sleepless night
In which I rolled frustrated and I smelt
Lust on myself, then smoke, and then I felt
Street bonfires blazing for the end of war
V.E. and J. burn us like lights, but saw
Lush prairies for a tumble, wide corrals,
A Loiner's Elysium, and I cried
For the family still pent up in my balls,
For my corned beef sandwich, and for genocide.

Doodlebugs

Even the Vicar teaching Classics knows
how the doodled prepuce finishes as man,
a lop-eared dachshund with a pubis nose,
Caspar the friendly ghost or Ku-Klux-Klan,
and sees stiff phalluses in lynched negroes,
the obvious banana, those extra twirls
that make an umbilicus brave mustachios
clustered round cavities no longer girls'.

Though breasts become sombreros, groins goatees,
the beard of Conrad, or the King of Spain,
bosoms bikes or spectacles, vaginas psis,
they make some fannies Africa, and here it's plain,
though I wonder if the Vicar ever sees,
those landmass doodles show a boy's true bent
for adult exploration, the slow discovery
of cunt as coastline, then as continent.

The White Queen

1. *Satyrae*

I

Professor! Poet! Provincial Dadaist!
Pathic, pathetic, half-blind and half-pissed
Most of these tours in Africa. A Corydon
Past fifty, fat, those suave looks gone,
That sallow cheek, that young Novello sheen
Gone matt and puffed. A radiant white queen
In sub-Saharan scrub, I hold my court
On expat pay, my courtiers all bought.

Dear Mother, with your hennaed hair and eyes
Of aquamarine, I made this compromise
With commodities and cash for you, and walk
These hot-house groves of Academe and talk
Nonsense and nothing, bored with almost all
The issues but the point of love. Nightfall
Comes early all year round. I am alone,
And early all year round I go to town
And grub about for love. I sometimes cruise
For boys the blackness of a two-day bruise,
Bolt upright in the backseat of the *Volks*,
Or, when the moon's up full, take breathless walks
Past leprosarium and polo grounds
Hedged with hibiscus, and go my rounds
Of downtown dance and bar. Where once they used
To castrate eunuchs to be shipped off East,
I hang about *The Moonshine* and *West End*,
Begging for pure sex, one unembarrassed friend
To share my boredom and my bed – *One masta want
One boy – one boy for bed* . . . and like an elephant
That bungles with its trunk about its cage,
I make my half-sloshed entrances and rage

Like any normal lover when I come
Before I've managed it. Then his thin bum
That did seem beautiful will seem obscene;
I'm conscious of the void, the *Vaseline*,
Pour shillings in his hands and send him back
With the driver, ugly, frightened, black,
Black, black. What's the use? I can't escape
Our foul conditioning that makes a rape
Seem natural, if wrong, and love unclean
Between some ill-fed blackboy and fat queen.

Things can be so much better. Once at least
A million per cent. Policeman! Priest!
You'll call it filthy, but to me it's love,
And to him it was. It *was*. O he could move
Like an oiled (slow-motion) racehorse at its peak,
Outrageous, and not gentle, tame, or meek –
O magnificently shameless in his gear,
He sauntered the flunkied restaurant, queer
As a clockwork orange and not scared.
God, I was grateful for the nights we shared.
My boredom melted like small cubes of ice
In warm sundowner whiskies. Call it vice;
Call it obscenity; it's love; so there;
Call it what you want. *I just don't care.*

Two figures in grey uniforms and shorts,
Their eyes on quick promotion and the tarts,
Took down the number of my backing car.
I come back raddled to the campus bar
And shout out how I laid a big, brute
Negro in a tight, white cowboy suit.

II

Advanced psychology (of 1910)
Bristled from thin lips the harmattan
Had cracked and shrivelled like a piece of bark.
She egged me on to kiss her in the scented dark,

Eyes bottled under contact lenses, bright
And boggling, as if for half the night
She'd puffed cheap hashish to console
Her for the absences, that great, black hole
Pascal had with him once, *l'abîme ouvert*
He thought was special but is everywhere.
He cackles from Heaven at the desperate Earth.

We permit ourselves too much satiric mirth
At their expense, and blame the climate, so
I touched her bosom gently just to show
I *could* acknowledge gestures, but couldn't stroke
Her leathery, dry skin and cracked a joke
Against myself about my taste in little boys.
Then the party drowned us in its noise
And carried us apart, I, to my jests,
She, to her gesturing with other guests.

I've seen her scrawny, listless husband still
Such rowdy booze-ups with a madrigal,
His tonic water serving for rare wine
Toasting the ladies with *O Mistress Mine*;
Sort of impressive. I confess such prick
Songs make me absolutely bloody sick,
But he can sing them straight at his *third* wife.
Changey-changey! But they can't change life,
Though they meditate together with joined hands,
Though his psyche flutters when he thinks he's kissed
Cuddled and copulated with New Zealand's
Greatest, unpublished, *woman* novelist.

III

All night a badly driven armoured truck
With grinding gears crunched on the gravel, shook
The loose louvres and the damp mosquito mesh,
And glaring headlights swept across my flesh.
Back to loneliness, pulling myself off,
After a whole *White Horse*, with photograph

And drag, a Livingstone with coloured plates,
That good old stand-by for expatriates
Hooked on the blacks; again have to withdraw
Into myself, backwards down a corridor,
Where in one of many cold, white cells
They play cold water on my testicles,
When I should be breaking out . . . must . . . must
Matchet the creeper from my strangled lust.

The sticky morning comes and some loud gun
Fires short distance shells into the sun.
Patrols and shots; the same trilingual drone
Goes on about curfews through a megaphone.
A new anthem: *tiddly-om-pom-pom*
Blares the new world like a Blackpool prom
And promises corruption's dead and lies
Riddled with bullets in three mortuaries.
An American's got it all on tape.
The proclamation: murder, looting, rape,
Homosexuality, all in the same breath,
And the same punishment for each – death, *death!*
He plays it back to half-seas-over, hushed
Circles in the bar. I flush with defiant lust.

Now life's as dizzy as the Book of Kells.
Thank God for London and Beaux/Belles.
I must get back again. I must, but must
Never again be locked away or trussed
Like a squealing piglet because my mind
Shut out all meaning like a blackout blind.

Next door, erotomaniacs. Here, queers,
And butch nurses with stiff hoses mock
As we grow limp, *Roundheads* and *Cavaliers*,
Like King Charles bowing to the chopping block.

IV

Insects strike the clapper. The school bell
Clangs for nothing. Nothing; and her little hell

Begins when darkness falls. Her garden moves
With mambas, leafage like damp leather gloves,
Cobras, rats and mice, and bandicoots,
The drunk *maigardai* and their prostitutes
Who help them pass their watch. Time drags
For such lonely, unlovable old bags.
There's too much spawning. Men! Beasts! Ticks!
Spawn in their swarmfuls like good Catholics.

She wanted children but she gets instead
Black houseboys leaving notes beside her bed:
Madam your man is me. Where is the yes?
Putting pressed frangipani in her dress.
She's not as desperate for a go as that.
She has her gaudy parrot and her spayed, grey cat
For company. *Babar*'s a champion impressionist
Of whisky noises when his owner's pissed.
She pretends he's learnt it when he's heard her wash
And offers visitors a choice of squash.

Darkness. The swoosh of soda and the glug
Of Scotch come from *Babar* as that drunken thug
She hired as a watchman and *must* fire, treads
Down her phlox and pees on her arctotis beds.
She knows what he's up to. Brute! The garage door
Swings on its hinges for the watchman's whore.
And now they're rocking. One cracked heel
Scrapes after purchase on her *Peugeot* wheel.
Rustle and gasp, black creatures claw
At one another in her packing straw.
You never know in these hot climates; *coups*
Can throw the whole white quarter on the booze.
Whisky and danger. Ah who knows? Who knows?
Some drunken Public Works might still propose.
But she wouldn't have him. No, not her. Boy!
She'll give you the sack for those grunts of joy.

V

Northwards two hundred miles, an emptiness
As big as Europe; *Sah'ra*; Nothingness.
South six hundred, miles of churning sea
Make of the strongest swimmer a nonentity,
Bleaching the blackest flesh as white as spray.
The sea makes no demands but gets its way.

The campus wants its pep- and sleeping pills.
It's not diseases, but the void that kills,
The space, the gaps, the darkness, that same void
He hears vibrating in clogged adenoid
And vocal cords. Through his cool stethoscope
He hears despair pulsate and withered hope
Flutter the failing heart a little, death
Of real feeling in a laboured breath.
He knows with his firm finger on a pulse
It is this Nothingness and nothing else
Throbs in the blood. Nothing is no little part
Of time's huge effort in the human heart.
There's love. There's courage. And that's all.
And the *itus et reditus* of Pascal.

He's not asked out to drinks or dinner much.
He knows how the slightest sweatrash on the crutch
Scares some and with good reason, whose child's whose,
Whose marriage depends on sjamboks, and who screws
In *Posts & Telegraphs*, and reads instead
His damp-stained *Pensées* on their double bed.
The Nothingness! Lisa – she couldn't stand
The boredom and packed off for Switzerland.
She sends him a postcard of a snowblown slope:
Boris, ich bin frei . . . und friere. He can't cope
Here alone. There's nothing for a sick MO
Sick of savannah, sick of inselberg,
Sick of black Africa, who cannot go
Ever again to white St Petersburg.

2. *The Railroad Heroides*

I

A lake like lead. A bar. The crowding, nude
Slack-breasted, tattooed girls made lewd,
Lascivious gestures, their bald groins
Studded with wet francs, for my loose coins.
I'm surrounded by canoes. *Cadeau! Cadeau!*
I fling out all my change, but they won't go.
One paddles underneath and pokes a straw
At my bare ankles through the gaping floor.
I'm on my fifth warm beer. I need my cash.
I crunch her knuckles hard, and yell out: *Vache!*
Then as she pulls my sandals: *Tu, vache noire!*
They rock the rotten stilts that prop the bar.
My boatman saves me, and for ten francs more
Canoes me blushing to the nearest shore.
I lie back like a corpse Valhalla bound
And sleep. Only a wet, withdrawal sound
Sucks at my ear. I dream. I dream the sun
Blackens my bare balls to bitumen.

II

Again I feel my school belt with the snake-
Hook, silver buckle tauten and then break
From the banisters I swung off. Suicide –
The noose's love-bites and a bruised backside.
I laughed a long time and was glad I fell.
The white wake swabbing at the woundless swell,
The swashing, greasy pool, the spindrift fine
As *Shelltox* seasoning my lips with brine
Makes sadness shoreless and shakes sullen grief
Apart like gobs of spittle. Off Tenerife
French soldiers from Gabon dressed up as sheikhs
Waltzed amidships and blackamoors cut cakes
Iced thick with tricolours. The *Marseillaise*
Boomed from the tannoy and the easy lays

Beamed at the officers. I flung your zig-zag
Tuareg ring and the red, goat-leather bag
I'd bought for our swimming things into the sea
Placating nothing. A little lighter, free
To saunter in fancy dress the festooned decks,
In the midst of plenty, hungry for good sex,
I found a lonely woman. I got you off my chest,
But had to have my hand held and I lay
All night with my confessor, fully dressed,
Afraid of my terror, longing for the day.

III

Bordeaux – Paris – London – Leeds; I get
Cold and tachycardia in my couchette.
With weeks of travel thudding in my brain,
Bilges, ship's engine, and the English train,
Too much black coffee and cold lager beer
I find sleep impossible. My throbbing ear
Bangs on the pillow with an angry thud –
It's you, it's you, with a sound like blood,
After the bloodshed, if your tribe survives,
Pounding a big man's yams among young wives.

IV

Leeds City Station, and a black man sweeps
Cartons and papers into tidy heaps.

3. *Travesties*

'. . . the vanity of translation; it were as wise to cast a pansy into a crucible that you might discover the formal principle of its colour and odour, as seek to transfuse from one language into another the creations of a poet.'

(Shelley, *A Defence of Poetry*)

Distant Ophir
(after Hieronymi Fracastorii, *Syphilis, sive Morbus Gallicus*, Veronae, MDXXX)

'Westerners, who laid the Sun's fowl low,
the flocks of Apollo, now stand and hear
the dreadful sufferings you must undergo.

This land, where you are now, is that Ophir
your flashy maps show off like jewellery
but not yet yours to own, nor domineer

its quiet peoples until now quite free;
cities and new sacraments you won't impose
until you've suffered much by land and sea.

Self-lumbered pilgrims of San Lazaro's,
brothels and gold bars bring you no joy,
porphyry and rape bring no repose!

You'll war with strangers, bloodily, destroy
or be destroyed, your discoveries will cost
destructions greater than the siege of Troy,

worse wanderings after with more thousands lost,
comrades you fitted out search parties for
hutches of bleached ribs on our bare coast.

You'll go on looking, losing more and more
to the sea, the climate, weapons, ours *and* yours,
your crimes abroad brought home as civil war.

And also *Syphilis*: sores, foul sores
will drive you back through storm and calenture
crawling like lepers to our peaceful shores.

The malaise of the West will lure
the scapegoats of its ills, you and your crew,
back to our jungles looking for a cure. –

You'll only find the Old World in the New,
and you'll rue your *discubrimiento*, rue
it, rue Africa, rue Cuba, rue Peru!'

And away behind the crags the dark bird flew.

And everything it prophesied came true.

Note. Hieronymus Fracastorius (1483–1553), the author of *Syphilis*,
was born, as perhaps befits a true poet, without a mouth. The fact is
celebrated in the well-known epigram of Julius Caesar Scaliger (1484–
1558). Fracastorius died, after an apoplexy, speechless.

4. *Manica*

'An experienced doctor has said that he has never seen tropical
neurasthenia develop in a man with a sound philosophy of life.'

(*Notes on the Preservation of Personal Health in Warm Climates*, London,
The Ross Institute of Tropical Hygiene, 3rd ed., 1960)

1. *The Origin of the Beery Way*

The Coast, the Coast, a hundred years ago!
Poisonous mangroves and funereal palms,
Victorian hearse-plumes nodding victims in
To bouts of wifeless boredom and *El Vomito*,
Shacking with natives, lovely Sodom's sin,
Boozers with riff-raff in their *British* arms.
Reports put down 'futility & worthlessness' –
I'm just a big *colon*: kick, kick, caress,
Administer, then murmur *beau, beau, beau*
Like some daft baby at your Mandingo.
From *dashi, dashi* to *cadeau, cadeau*,
Armed with my *Dettol*, my *Od-o-ro-no*,
My *African Personality*, I go
For a bit of the old Français finesse,
Not work at your ballocks like a kid's yo-yo,
Then buck you off them like a rodeo.
With prudish pansies I am passionless.
My sex-life's manic like a bad rondeau.
I need to forage among Francophones.
A real beaubarian and buckaneer, that's me, Yo Ho,
Bottles of *Black & White* do me for rum.
I soft-shoe shuffle on the white man's bones,
Windborne or brittle as a popadum.

Omar, not Khayam, the Gambia's mad Marabout
Changed the Commissioners' bullets into water;
Into water being Moslem. I, being atheist,
Am full of more potent potions when I'm pissed.

A century later, full of *Guinnesses* and *Stars*,
I'm God's own Heaven, and as I slash I shout:
The white man's water turns back into fire!
Braving castration at their scimitars,
And single-handed put Islam to rout,
And vanquish the missions with my bent desire,
Spouting a semen capable of slaughter.

Flat on my back, beneath the Galaxy, I fear
This burning in my groin is gonorrhoea.

II. *The Elephant & the Kangaroo*

The first rains slap the leaves like slow applause.
My nerves are soothed by it.
The insects' constant grind has been put down.
It means a night indoors;
nothing doing in the town;
power failure; all the dives unlit.

The imported apples begin to look like shit.
The *Star* beer's warmish, the cut fruit brown.
Chops will be rotting in the Lebanese Cold Stores.
The rainmaker wraps away his amulet
and hugs his gods to see the great downpours.

So the world comes back into its own
and all the houses through a stage-scene gauze
of wavering, driven rain and drunkenness. *It*
goes on spinning and will not run down.
In cool bush-shirt and shorts I sit
feeling the world spinning, the spinning floors
between the brandy and verandah. Laterite.
Bush, like effigies of bush, is washed of it.
A clean green everywhere and it still pours.
This is Noah's weather. All will drown –

But I'll escape by crawling on all fours.

III. *The Foreign Body*

Each blue horizontal thrust
into the red, rain-spattered dust
brings my tachycardia back.
My heart's a thing caught in a sack.
Lashes of tall grass whip
at my genitals, the thick ears flip
hard insects from sprung stalks
and the fraying lightning forks.
Boom! The flame trees blaze
out the ancientest of days.
All the dead in running shoes!
A bootless marchpast of dead Jews!
Boom! Bad blood cells boom
in unison for *Lebensraum*.
Burst corpuscles and blood cells spray
the dark with fire and die away.
The brief glares strewed
flamboyants in my face like blood.
Boom! Boom! And at each wrist
a worm as blue as amethyst
burrows its blunt head in my palm
to keep its bloodless body warm.

And in my bed I hear the whine
of soliciting anopheline,
and diptera diseases zoom
round and round my foetid room,
and randiness, my life's disease,
in bottle green Cantharides,
and the bloody tampan, that posh louse
plushy like an Opera House,
red as an Empire or lipstick,
insect vampire, soft-backed tick –
all females, the female womb
is stuffed with blind trypanosome.
Which of your probosces made

my heart fire off this cannonade,
or is its billion gun salute
for lover or for prostitute?
Boom! Boom! And now here comes
the endless roll of danger drums,
and the death-defying leap
jerks me panicking from sleep.
Boom! Boom! Bonhomie!
America's backslapping me.
Starchy Baptist cherubim
give me tests at the SIM,
and swallowed US tracers trace
my body's Cuban missile base.
Boom! Boom! World War 3's
waging in my arteries.

Desperately I call these app-
rehensions Africa but the map
churns like wet acres in these rains
and thunder tugging at my veins.
That Empire flush diluted is
pink as a lover's orifice,
then *Physical*, *Political* run
first into marblings and then one
mud colour, the dirty, grey,
flat reaches of infinity.

The one red thing, I squat and grab
at myself like a one-clawed crab.

5. *from* The Zeg-Zeg Postcards

I

Africa – London – Africa –
to get it away.

II

My white shorts tighten
in the market crowds.
I don't know
if a lean Fulani boy
or girl gave me this stand
trailing his/her knuckles
on my thigh.

III

Knowing my sense of ceremonial
my native tailor
still puts
buttons on my flies.

IV

I bought three *Players* tins
of groundnuts with green mould
just to touch your hand
counting the coppers into mine.

V

My Easter weekend Shangri-la, Pankshin.
I watch you pour the pure
well water, balanced up the mountain,
in blinding kerosene cans,
each lovely morning, convict,
your release date, nineteen years from now,
daubed in brown ink on your rotting shirt.

VI

My *White Horse* plastic horses carousel
whirls round an empty and my hell,
when the last neat whisky passes my cracked lips,
is a riderless Apocalypse.

VII *Water Babies*

She hauls at his member like a crude *shaduf*
to give her dry loins life, and calls it love.

She's back in England pregnant. Now he can
flood the damned valley of his African.

VIII

Sex beefs at belled virginity. The wives
nag back at sex. Ding, Dong! Ding, Dong!
rings no changes on their married lives
clapping out *Love's Old Sweet Song*.

What's that to me? I can get a stand
even from maps of the Holy Land.

IX

Je suis le ténébreux . . . le veuf . . .
always the *soixante* and never the *neuf*.

X

It's time for tea and biscuits. No one comes.
I hear the flap of Dunlop sandals, drums,
terrifying cries. My clap still bothers me.
Siestas make me dizzy. I stagger up and see
through mesh and acacia sharp metal flash,
my steward, still in white uniform and sash,
waving a sharpened piece of Chevie, ride
his old *Raleigh* to the genocide.

XI

The shower streams over him
and the water turns instantly
to cool *Coca-Cola*.

XII

We shake baby powder over each other
like men salting a spitroast,
laughing like kids in a sandpit,
childish ghosts of ourselves,
me, puffy marshmallow, he,
sherbert dusted liquorice
licked back bright
and leading into *Turkish Delight*.

XIII

Buttocks. Buttocks.
You pronounce it as though
the syllables rhymed: *loo*; *cocks*.
I murmur over and over:
buttocks . . . buttocks . . . BUTOX,
marketable essence of beef –
négritude – dilute to taste!

XIV

I'd like to
sukuru
you.

XV

Mon égal!
Let me be the Gambia
in your Senegal.

The Heart of Darkness

Disjointed like a baobab,
gigantic first, then noonday blob,
my shadow staggers, lurches, reels,
elasticated at my heels,
then stretches out with its blind reach
way beyond the gasp of speech.
The wind's up and our last weak light
dithers and lets in the night.

Shadowless, one dark hand flits
spiderwise for crusted bits
of Christmas candle, German *art-
creation* wax with plastic Chartres
Cathedral windows, coloured light
evoking Europe till Twelfth Night
and aspirations from our dust
with no repository but lust.

Earthed so, lust like radar beams
bleeps for realities from dreams
out of darkness for the new, rich life,
the unmistakable pulsation – wife,
my blurred light in the blind
concentric circles of blank mind,
this blackout makes our flesh and bone
an Africa, a Livingstone.

Like galoshes going *vitch* . . .
vitch . . . an Easter birch switch
going *vitch* . . . the fan slows
down and stops, dense mangoes
rustle and a Congo band sings
indigenous and Western things.
The crowds flock in, agog to feel
new *frissons* out of Brazzaville.

Novelties! Good drummers come
miles to hear a different drum
as men go to adulteries. Sounds!
Women! It's the same. Our ground's
stamped and rutted, so we choose
either to hog it in squelched ooze,
or get resurrection and find sties
most radiant with novelties.

My shadow's back as if it could
smell lust steaming off my blood:
Fee, Fi, Fo, Fum,
this is my *Praeconium*.
Paging angels set down this
fastidious and human kiss;
and this; and this; and this; and set
down this, my *Exultet*:

Everything in this rich dark
craves my exclamation mark.
Wife! Mouth! Breasts! Thigh!
certe necessarium Adae
peccatum . . . felix culpa . . . O felix
dark continent of fallen sex.
Harrowing Christ! O Superlamb,
grown lupine, luminous – *Shazam*!

Not so bravado now, but bare
cold, and sober on a camel-hair
Saharan blanket. Tuareg guards
patrolling with their rusty swords
swing up a lamp and weldmesh
thief-bars check our flesh
gleaming: breasts; thigh; bum;
out of our aquarium.

Our fruitless guava quincunx
curvets on its supple trunks.
The candles in the empties flare

sideways in the stirring air
and then go out. The curtains soar
horizontal with the floor.
It seems a whole sea must pour through
our all-glass house at Samaru.

And now all's dark and the first rains
splatter at the window panes,
flattening down ten rows of beans,
a bed of radishes. This means
no news from England, no new war
to heighten the familiar:
Nigeria's Niger is not yet
harnessed to our wireless set.

The Songs of the PWD Man

'We were not born to survive, alas,
But to step on the gas.'
                    (Andrei Voznesensky)

I

I'll bet you're bloody jealous, you codgers in UK,
Waiting for your hearses while I'm having it away
With girls like black Bathshebas who sell their milky
    curds
At kerbside markets out of done-up-fancy gourds,
Black as tar-macadam, skin shining when it's wet
From washing or from kissing like polished Whitby jet.
They're lovely, these young lasses. Those colonial DO's
Knew what they were up to when they upped and chose
These slender, tall Fulanis like Rowntrees coffee creams
To keep in wifeless villas. No Boy Scout's fleapit dreams
Of bedding Brigitte Bardot could ever better these.
One shy kiss from this lot has me shaking at the knees.
It's not that they're casual, they're just glad of the lifts
I give them between markets and in gratitude give gifts
Like sips of fresh cow-juice off a calabash spoon.
But I'm subject to diarrhoea, so I'd just as soon
Have a feel of those titties that hang down just below
That sort of beaded bolero of deep indigo blue;
And to the woven wrapper worn exactly navel high,
All's bare but for ju-jus and, where it parts, a thigh
Sidles through the opening with a bloom like purple
    grapes.
So it's not all that surprising that some lecherous apes
Take rather rough advantage, mostly blacks and Leban-
    ese,
Though I've heard it tell as well that it were one of these
That *white* Police Inspector fancied and forced down
At the back of barracks in the sleazy part of town.

Well, of course, she hollered and her wiry brothers ran
And set rabid packs of bushdogs on the desperate man.
He perished black all over and foaming at the mouth.
They're nomadic, these Fulanis, driving to the South
That special hump-backed cow they have, and when
  they're on trek,
They leave wigwamloads of women, and by blooming
  heck,
    drive in their direction, my right foot pressed right
    down
Laying roads and ladies up as far as Kano town.
Though I'm not your socialistic, go-native-ite type chap
With his flapping, nig-nog dresses and his dose of clap,
I have my finer feelings and I'd like to make it clear
I'm not just itchy fingers and a senile lecher's leer.
I have my qualms of conscience and shower *silver*, if you
  please,
To their lepers and blind beggars kipping under trees.
They're agile enough, those cripples, scrabbling for the
  coins,
But not half so bloody agile as those furry little groins
I grope for through strange garments smelling of dye-
  pits
As I graze my grizzly whiskers on those black, blancmangy
  tits.
I don't do bad for sixty. You can stuff your Welfare
  State.
You can't get girls on National Health and I won't mas-
  turbate.
They're pleased with my performance. I'm satisfied with
  theirs.
No! I think they're very beautiful, although their hair's
A bit off-putting, being rough like panscrub wires,
But bums like melons, matey, lips like lorry tyres.
They all know old Roller Coaster. And, oh dear, ugh!
To think I ever nuzzled on a poor white woman's dug,
Pale, collapsed and shrivelled like a week-old mushroom
  swept

Up at Kirkgate City Markets. Jesus bleeding wept!
Back to sporting, smoky Yorkshire! I dread retirement
  age
And the talking drum send-off at the Lagos landing
  stage.

Out here I'm as sprightly as old George Formby's uke.
I think of Old Folk's England and, honest, I could puke.
Here I'm getting younger and I don't need monkey
  glands,
Just a bit of money and a pair of young, black hands.
I used to cackle at that spraycart trying to put down
That grass and them tansies that grew all over town.
Death's like the Corporation for old men back in Leeds,
Shooting out its poisons and choking off the weeds.
But I'm like them tansies or a stick cut in the bush
And shoved in for a beanpole that suddenly grows lush
With new leafage before the garden lad's got round
To plucking the beans off and digging up the ground.
Yes, better to put the foot down, go fast, accelerate,
Than shrivel on your arses, mope and squawk and wait
For Death to drop the darkness over twittering age
Like a bit of old blanket on a parrot's cage.

II

Life's movement and life's danger and not a sit-down
  post.
There's skeleton cars and lorries from Kano to the coast;
Skeletons but not wasted, those flashy Chevie fins
Honed up for knife blades or curled for muezzins
To megaphone the *Koran* from their mud mosques and
  call
The sun down from its shining with their caterwaul.
But it's not just native say-so; it's stark, realistic fact;
The road's a royal python's dark digestive tract.
And I expect that it'll get me one rainy season night,
That sudden, skating backwheel skid across the laterite,
Or a lorry without headlights, GOD IS LOVE up on the cab,

Might impale me on my pistons like a raw *kebab*.
Smash turned into landscape, ambulance, that's that,
A white corpse starkers like a suddenly skinned cat.

As kids when we came croppers, there were always some
    old dears
Who'd come and pick us up and wipe off blood and
    tears,
And who'd always use the same daft words, as they tried
    to console,
Pointing to cobble, path or flagstone: *Look at the hole
You've made falling.* I want a voice with that soft tone,
Disembodied Yorkshire like my mother's on the phone,
As the cook puts down some flowers and the smallboy
    scrapes the spade,
To speak as my epitaph: *Look at the hole he's made.*

The Death of the PWD Man

'Chivo que rompe tambor con su pellejo paga.'

(Abakuá proverb)

I

Earth-brown Garden Bulbuls in the Bathurst graveyard trees
Sing, they say, 'quick-doctor-quick' or 'fifty-nine degrees'.
God knows, but I'm drawn to graves like brides to babywear
Spending an afternoon ashore to see who's buried there.
Ozanne, DO Blackwater Fever. FAITHFUL UNTO DEATH.
A commissioner, they say, who mustered his last breath
And went on chanting till he croaked the same damn thing:
A coffle of fourteen asses bound for Sansanding!
Then *Leeds* medic Rothery Adgie, dead at twenty six,
His barely legible wooden cross a bundle of split sticks.
Though mostly nineteen hundreds half the graves have gone
Succumbing like the men below to rains and harmattan.
But fine windborne sand and downpours can't obliterate
BLAKEBOROUGH'S (BRIGHOUSE) from the iron hydrant grate
Outside the Residence, and I've a sense of dismal pride
Seeing Yorkshire linger where ten Governors have died.
The same as in Nigeria, though the weather rots the cross,
There's HUNSLET (LEEDS) in iron on an engine up at Jos.

Wintering house-martins flutter round MacCarthy Square
And bats from Mauritanian shops get tangled in your hair.
Sunset; six; the muezzin starts calling; church bells clang,

Swung iron against iron versus amplified *Koran*.
It's bottoms up at sundown at the praying ground and
    bar,
Though I prefer the bottle to the Crescent and the Star,
The bottle to the Christians' Cross, and, if I may be
    frank,
Living to all your Heavens like a woman to a wank.
And it's a bottle that I'm needing as I get back to the boat
With a lump like coal or iron sticking in my throat.
Though I take several bottles, though I hawk like hell
    and cough,
It stays fixed like a lodestone Northwards as the boat
    casts off.

II

Sunday Scotsman Northwards, autumn trees all rusting
    up;
My fifth *Light Ale* is swashing in its BR plastic cup.
Coming back to England; there's no worse way than this
Railroad North from London up to *Worstedopolis*.
Britannia, Old Mother Riley, bending down to pray,
The railway line's the X-Ray of her twisted vertebrae.
I'm watching England rolling by; here a startled grouse
Shoots out from a siding, and there Sabbath-idle ploughs
Clogged in soggy furrows are seizing up with rain.
Life's either still or scurrying away from the train.

Anxious, anxious, anxious, anxious, perhaps the train'll
    crash.
Anxious, anxious, anxious, Doctor Adgie, there's a rash
The shape of bloody Britain and it's starting to spread.
My belly's like a blow-up globe all blotched with Empire red.
Chancres, chancres, Shetlands, spots, boils, Hebrides,
Atlasitis, Atlasitis, British Isles Disease!

The rot sets in at Retford and the stations beyond;
Coffles of coupled, rusty coaltrucks chalkmarked COND.
But at each abandoned station shunned like a suicide

There's that loveliest of flourishers, the purple *London Pride*.

Though why the 'proud' metropolis should monopolize weeds

Beats me, when we've got millions more all over mucky Leeds,

Springing up wherever life is teetering on the brink

Like pensioned-off yours truly's pickled in his drink.

With a bit of help off Bitter, I can do it on my own.

They can stuff their pink *Somalgins* and their *Phenobarbitone*,

O those lovely bubs that almost touched black chin and shiny knees,

Leaping up and down to drumming like hoop-jumping Pekinese!

Ay, it's a pity all that's over. From now on every night

It's *Whatsoever Thy Hand Findeth To Do, Do It With Thy Might*.

Anxious, anxious, anxious, anxious, perhaps the train'll crash.

Anxious, anxious, anxious, Doctor Adgie, there's a rash

The shape of bloody Britain and it's starting to spread.

My belly's like a blow-up globe all blotched with Empire red.

Chancres, chancres, Shetlands, spots, boils, Hebrides,

Atlasitis, Atlasitis, British Isles Disease.

Veni, vidi, vici, Death's cackling in my ear.

And there he is a Caesar with an earth-caked Roman spear.

Queer sorts of dozes these are, where I'm nodding off to dream

Of being chased by Caesars and I wake up with a scream.

Must be that pork-pie I've eaten or the British Railways Ale.

Night behind the window. My coaster's tan gone deathly pale.

It's *me!* It's *me* the fauna's fleeing. Nothing'll keep still.

My adrenalin moves Nature now and not God's heavenly
will.
Lean closer as the darkness grows. My vision's fogged by
breath
Clouding up the window as life's clouded up by death.

Anxious, anxious, anxious, anxious, perhaps the train'll
crash
Anxious, anxious, anxious, Doctor Adgie, there's a rash
The shape of bloody Britain and it's starting to spread.
My belly's like a blow-up globe all blotched with Empire red.
Chancres, chancres, Shetlands, spots, boils, Hebrides,
Atlasitis, Atlasitis, British Isles Disease.

Death's chuntered in my ear-hole since I was thirty five,
And I've guffawed at his stories but I've kept myself
alive
Long enough to get fed up of the same old, worn-out
joke.
Death, piss off, you shaggy dog, you proper natterpoke!
Nay! Come on, Julius Seizure, you black, buck bastard
come.
I can hear those muffled heartbeats like a Yoruba
drum.
And see the curving shadow of the sinister drumstick,
A bit of whittling that depicts an old man's drooping
prick,
Poised above the tautened heart, on the point of being
played,
Just once, just once, and then I join the goners' masquer-
ade.

Anxious, anxious, anxious, anxious, perhaps the train'll
crash.
Anxious, anxious, anxious, Doctor Adgie, there's a rash
The shape of bloody Britain and it's starting to spread.
My belly's like a blow-up globe all blotched with Empire red.
Chancres, chancres, Shetlands, spots, boils, Hebrides,
Atlasitis, Atlasitis, British Isles Disease.

My transparent head and shoulders ringed with reading
   lights
Goes sliding over hillsides, graveyards, demolition sites.
I'm a sort of setting sun, all my light drawn in to shed
Only darkness on the living, only darkness on the dead.
Life the bright compartment between dark cattle trucks
Concertinaed in the crush like a bug between two books.
Night and silence, and the Scotsman rushing, second
Coupled to anxious, anxious SE*cond* . . . COND . . .
   COND . . . COND . . .

Schwiegermutterlieder

I

Mother and daughter German refugees
were not much wanted in nineteen
forty five. She had to skivvy for rich Jews
in Manchester's posh 'Palestine'.

I never really could believe
her story of your being thrown out
by some, one *snowy* Christmas Eve,
for having real wax candles on your conifer,
their children shouting: *Kraut! Kraut!*
until she brought the tea-chests out of store.

Then I saw the hotel towels, the stolen
London café spoons,
bits of half-eaten *Stollen*,
casserole and cooking pans
packed hot from the oven.

Kleptomaniac,
dear *Schwiegermutter*,
did you have to pack
a ½lb Kosher butter?

I've seen her waltz
off with rare, bright plants she's pinched
from Kew, but the good bed-linen
was her own, brought bunched
up in bundles from Berlin,
embroidered: *Mein Heim ist Mein Stolz*.

After 13 years she fished
out her treasures; none any use.
She gave us a perished
red-rubber douche.

After the wedding she insisted on
a head-and-shoulders photograph that just
got her *real* violets on your breast
but not your belly in.

She sang and spun round in a raven
black, hook-buttoned waitress dress.
She was in some sort of heaven,
Viennese with happiness,
her arms round everybody's neck,
warbling from pre-war musicals,
and *Rů-*, *Rů-*, *Růženka Maria*, your name in Czech,
with cracked ecstatic trills. –

But dying uncle Bertolt
made his '14–18 amputation tender
by stamping his tin foot, when he was told
you'd married an *Engländer*.

III

Else Crossfield, Dietzsch,
née Schubert – *British* bitch!

The Curtain Catullus

'Frontiers oppress me . . . I want to wander as much as I like . . .
to talk, even in a broken language, with everybody.'
(Yevtushenko, 1958)

Your fat, failed ballet dancer's calves
Bulge left, right, left. I'm out of breath and stop
To get a peep in at the skirted halves,
Those pale four inches past the stocking top.
That sight's more in my line. I'm not so sold
On all this Gothic and this old Baroque.
My fur hat tickles and I'm freezing cold.
I need a drink, a sit-down and a smoke.
I speak my one word of your language: *thanks!*
Let's kiss. You laugh and pivot on one toe
To point out Hus still preaching, Russian tanks,
And Kafka's ball-less eyes caked up with snow.

I glance round for my tail. We met head-on
In one blind alley, face to face. We grinned
And nodded and went on. I hope he's gone.
He'd shop us if he saw my bourgeois hand
Slide down the zip-line of your dress and pass
The vertebrae, your parted Party lips
Against my lips. Relax! No cause or class
Can take the pleasure from between your hips.

Astraea! Stalin's chocolate-Santa-Claus-
like statue's made piecemeal. Descend! Descend!
We're human, young, and lustful, sick of wars.
I want this gorgeous red bird for my friend.
Descend like a snow maiden from the air.
Fill Chrysostom's or Basil's empty niche,
Crumple stiff Nelson in Trafalgar Square.
Hear masses shouting: *Goddess!* bosses: *Bitch!*
We know you foreign Mata Hari whores.

I'm tired of stone bodies. I want yours.

Security's embarrassing, bored noise
Booms in these cracked cupolas: *Avoid,*
Avoid glad eyes, come–hithers, girl's or boy's.
Beware Caucasian and Mongoloid . . .
Above all, please remember Gerald Brooke.
O I could see the flags, red, white and blue,
And Red struck to half-mast for a fuck
Between a caught-out couple like us two.

Your body plumped by bread and dumplings strains
Against your imitation bearskin as you peer
Upwards at huge saints, your peach neck cranes
At some Church soldier launching a gold spear
Against the Turk. One lurking Infidel
Is herded by Christ's army into Hell.
I'm tired. Natasha! Olga! Masha! Come
To my bugged bedroom. Leave mausoleum,
Church, museum be. Leave your clothes there – Cold
  War
Bashing its dead torches on our door.

The Bedbug

Comrade, with your finger on the playback switch,
Listen carefully to each love-moan,
And enter in the file which cry is real, and which
A mere performance for your microphone.

Curtain Sonnets

1. *Guava Libre*

for Jane Fonda,
Leningrad, 1975

Pickled Gold Coast clitoridectomies?
Labia minora in formaldehyde?
A rose pink death mask of a screen cult kiss,
Marilyn's mouth or vulva mummified?

Lips cropped off a poet. That's more like.
That's almost the sort of poet I think I am.
The lips of Orpheus fished up by a dyke
singing 'Women of Cuba Libre and Vietnam!'

The taste, though, taste! Ah, that could only be

('Women! Women! O *abajo* men,
the thought of it's enough to make you come!')

the honeyed yoni of Eurydice

and I am Orpheus going down again –

Thanks for the guavas soaked in Cuban rum.

2. *The Viewless Wings*

(Monkwood, Grimley)

The hungry generations' new decree
turns Worcester orchards into fields of sage.

Tipsy, courtesy cheap wine and EEC,
I hear, as unaware of ours as Keats's age,
the same blithe bird but its old magic fails
and my longing for you now is just as bad
at England's northern edge for nightingales
as those White Nights last year in Leningrad,
where, packed for my flight back, thick curtains drawn
but night too like full day to get much kip,
I wanted you to watch with me from bed
that seamless merger of half dusk and dawn,
AURORA, rosy-fingered kind, and battleship
whose sudden salvo turned the East half red.

3. *Summer Garden*

Winter false dawns woke me: *thud! thud! thud!*
Lorries loaded with chipped ice and not quite four!
Felt-swathed babushkas stooping to chip more –
Leningrad's vast pool of widowhood,
who also guard the Rembrandts and rank Gents,
who stand all day with stern unbending gaze
haloed with Tsars' crowns and Fabergés,
their menfolk melted down to monuments.

It's their eyes make me shy I've fallen for
a woman who they'd chorus at *nyet! nyet!*
and make me edgy walking here with you
between the statues VERITAS, HONOR,
and PSYCHE whom strong passion made forget
conditions of darkness and the gods' taboo.

4. *The People's Palace*

Shuffling in felt goloshes saves the floor
from the unexpected guests of history
who queue all day to see what once was for
the fruits of just one bonsai family tree.

IUSTITIA and POMONA in their crates.
Come winter and the art, all cordoned off,
's wired to a US import anti-theft device
and opened only for researching prof.
and *patineur* from Academe who skates
those ballrooms patterned like cracked Baikal ice
buffing the princely parquets for the few
who'll see them reproduced in some review.

Watch that elegant glissade as he yahoos
into the soundproof pile of overshoes.

5. *Prague Spring*

on my birthday, 30 April

A silent scream? The madrigal's top note?
Puking his wassail on the listening throng?
Mouthfuls of cumulus, then cobalt throat.
Medusa must have hexed him in mid-song.

The finest vantage point in all of Prague's
this gagging gargoyle's with the stone-locked lute,
leaning over cherries, blow-ups of Karl Marx
the pioneers 'll march past and salute.

Tomorrow's May but still a North wind scuffs
the plated surface like a maced cuirass,
lays on, lays off, gets purchase on and roughs
up the Vltava, then makes it glass.

The last snow of this year's late slow thaw
dribbles as spring saliva down his jaw.

The Nuptial Torches

'These human victims, chained and burning at the stake, were the blazing torches which lighted the monarch to his nuptial couch.'

(J. L. Motley, *The Rise of the Dutch Republic*)

Fish gnaw the Flushing capons, hauled from fleeced
Lutheran Holland, for tomorrow's feast.
The Netherlandish lengths, the Dutch heirlooms,
That might have graced my movements and my groom's
Fade on the fat sea's bellies where they hung
Like cover-sluts. Flesh, wet linen wrung
Bone dry in a washerwoman's raw, red,
Twisting hands, bed-clothes off a lovers' bed,
Falls off the chains. At Valladolid
It fell, flesh crumpled like a coverlid.

Young Carlos de Sessa stripped was good
For a girl to look at and he spat like wood
Green from the orchards for the cooking pots.
Flames ravelled up his flesh into dry knots
And he cried at the King: *How can you stare
On such agonies and not turn a hair?*
The King was cool: *My friend, I'd drag the logs
Out to the stake for my own son, let dogs
Get at his testes for his sins; auto-da-fés
Owe no paternity to evil ways.*
Cabrera leans against the throne, guffaws
And jots down to the Court's applause
Yet another of the King's *bon mots*.

O yellow piddle in fresh fallen snow –
Dogs on the Guadarramas . . . dogs. Their souls
Splut through their pores like porridge holes.
They wear their skins like cast-offs. Their skin grows
Puckered round the knees like rumpled hose.

Doctor Ponce de la Fuente, you,
Whose gaudy, straw-stuffed effigy in lieu
Of members hacked up in the prison, burns
Here now, one sacking arm drops off, one turns
A stubble finger and your skull still croons
Lascivious catches and indecent tunes;
And croaks: *Ashes to ashes, dust to dust.*
Pray God be with you in your lust.
And God immediately is, but such a one
Whose skin stinks like a herring in the sun,
Huge from confinement in a filthy gaol,
Crushing the hooping on my farthingale.

O Holy Mother, Holy Mother, Ho-
ly Mother Church, whose melodious, low
Labour-moans go through me as you bear
These pitch-stained children to the upper air,
Let them lie still tonight, no crowding smoke
Condensing back to men float in and poke
Their charcoaled fingers at our bed, and let
Me be his pleasure, though Philip sweat
At his rhythms and use those hateful tricks
They say he feels like after heretics.

O let the King be gentle and not loom
Like Torquemada in the torture room,
Those wiry Spanish hairs, these nuptial nights,
Crackling like lit tapers in his tights,
His seed like water spluttered off hot stone.
Maria, whose dark eyes very like my own
Shine on such consummations, Maria bless
My Philip just this once with gentleness.

The King's cool knuckles on my smoky hair!

Mare Mediterraneum, la mer, la mer
That almost got him in your gorge with sides
Of feastmeats, you must flush this scared bride's
Uterus with scouring salt. O cure and cool
The scorching birthmarks of his branding-tool.

Sweat chills my small breasts and limp hands.

They curled like foetuses, *maman*, and cried.

His crusted tunics crumple as he stands:

Come, Isabella. God *is satisfied*.

Newcastle is Peru

'Correct your maps: Newcastle is Peru!'
                    (John Cleveland)

'Venient annis saecula seris,
Quibus Oceanus vincula rerum
Laxet & ingens pateat tellus,
Tethysque novos detegat orbes,
Nec sit terris ultima Thule.'
                    (Seneca, *Medea*, 375–9)

For defending in our Civil Wars
the King's against the better cause,
Newcastle got its motto: FORTIT-
ER TRIUMPHANS DEFENDIT.
After Nigeria and Prague I come
back near to where I started from,
all my defences broken down
on nine or ten *Newcastle Brown*.

A sudden, stiff September breeze
blows off the sea along the quays
and chills us; autumn and I need
your shoulder with a desperate need.
A clumsy effort at control,
I faff with paper chips and coal,
and rake out with elaborate fuss
one whole summer's detritus.

A good draught and the fire roars
like muted Disney dinosaurs,
and last week's Sunday paper glows
yellowish, its urgent prose,
like flies across a carcass, spreads
and fattens on the voiceless dead.

A picture shows lobbed mortar bombs
smashing down Onitsha homes.

The fire sucks in the first cold air
under the coverage of massacre.
The fire chatters, almost flies,
a full-fledged bird of paradise.
I lay down, dizzy, drunk, alone,
life circling life like the Eddystone
dark sea, but lighting nothing; sense
nor centre, nor circumference.

A life-long, sick sixpennyworth
of appalling motion round the Earth;
scared, moonrocketing till Pop-
eye and blurred planets stop;
Switchback; *Helter Skelter*; *Reel*;
the Blackpool Pleasure Beach Big Wheel,
its million coloured lightbulbs one
red halo like an empty sun.

The *Caterpillar*; Hunslet Feast;
one hand on my first woman's breast;
darkness; acceleration so
we're desperate with vertigo;
then chained in solitary *Chair-
o-planes* through whistling air
as all the known Leeds landmarks blur
to something dark and circular.

Venus, Vulcan, Cupid stare
out vacantly on City Square,
and *Deus iuvat impigros*
above the bank where God helps those
who help themselves, declares
Leeds purposeful in its affairs.
Mercator; *miles*, school chapel glass
transparencies to blood and brass.

And *Self Help* Samuel Smiles was said
to have waltzed round our first bed
in our partitioned ballroom flat
with hardly room to swing a cat.
Worthies! Loiners! O King Dick
Oastler and his rhetoric,
and William Hey, the first to show
syphilis *in utero*.

O highlife crocodiles that went
round one palm tree in the bare cement!
The dizziness! That spiral stair
up St Vitus's Cathedral; there
the golden cockerel and great Prague
before us like a catalogue;
slides. Bloodless mementos, all
Time-Life International.

And now with vistas like Earl Grey's
I look out over life and praise
from my unsteady, sea-view plinth
each dark turn of the labyrinth
that might like a river suddenly
wind its widening banks into the sea
and Newcastle is Newcastle is New-
castle *is* Peru!

Swirled detritus and driftwood pass
in state the 1880 *Sas-
inena Cold Storage Co.*,
and Neptune gazes at the Tyne's flow
seawards, where the sea-winds 'boast
and bluster' at the North East coast,
the sluggish Tyne meandering through
the staithes and shipyards of Peru.

Shadow girders faced with sun
shimmer like heaped bullion.
Commerce and contraceptives glide
and circle on the turning tide;

Plain, *Gossamer* and *Fetherlite*
and US *Trojan*, knotted tight,
ferry their unborn semen, free
for ever from discovery.

Discovery! Slaves, now trains,
like *spirochetes* through dark brains,
tunnel the Andes, spiralling for zinc
and silver, gold and lead; drink
still makes me giddy; my mind whirls
through all my wanderings and girls
to one last city, whose black crest
shows all the universe at rest.

At rest! That last red flash
as life's last ember turns to ash
and riddled dusts drop through the grate
around the heart. O celebrate,
as panic screws up each charged nerve
to cornering the next sharp swerve,
Earth, people, planets as they move
with all the gravity of love.

First this Victorian terrace, where
small scars of the last World War –
those wrought iron railings made
into shrapnel and grenade,
acanthus leaf and fleur-dé-lys,
victorious artillery –
are enough reminder that we brave
harsh opposition when we love.

This cluttered room, its chandelier
still spinning from the evening's beer,
this poor, embattled fortress, this strong-
hold of love, that can't last long
against the world's bold cannonade
of loveless warfare and cold trade,
this bed, this fire, and lastly us,
naked, bold, adventurous.

Discovery! wart, mole, spot,
like outcrops on a snowfield, dot
these slopes of flesh my fingers ski
with circular dexterity.
This moment when my hand strays
your body like an endless maze,
returning and returning, you,
O you; you also are Peru.

And just as distant. Flashing stars
drop to the ashpit through the bars.
I'm back in Africa, at ease
under the splashed shade of four trees,
watching a muscled woman heave
huge headloads of dead wood; one bare leaf
for covering wilts in the heat,
curls, then flutters to her flat, cracked feet.

And round each complex of thatched huts
is a man-high cactus hedge that shuts
out intruders and the mortars thud
like a migraine in the compound mud.
Night comes, and as drunk as hell
I watch the heavens and fireflies, and can't tell,
here at my Shangri-la, Pankshin,
where insects end and stars begin.

My fingerprints still lined with coal
send cold shudders through my soul.
Each whorl, my love-, my long life-line,
mine, inalienably mine,
lead off my body as they press
onwards into nothingness.
I see my grimy fingers smudge
everything they feel or touch.

The fire I laid and lit to draw
you downstairs to the second floor,
flickers and struts upon my bed.
And I'm left gazing at a full-page spread

of aggressively fine bosoms, nude
and tanned almost to *négritude*,
in the Colour Supplement's *Test
Yourself for Cancer of the Breast*.

Durham

'St Cuthbert's shrine,
founded 999'
                    (mnemonic)

ANARCHY and GROW YOUR OWN
whitewashed on to crumbling stone
fade in the drizzle. There's a man
handcuffed to warders in a black sedan.
A butcher dumps a sodden sack
of sheep pelts off his bloodied back,
then hangs the morning's killings out,
cup-cum-muzzle on each snout.

I've watched where this 'distinguished see'
takes off into infinity,
among transistor antennae,
and student smokers getting high,
and visiting Norwegian choirs
in raptures over Durham's spires,
lifers, rapists, thieves, ant-size
circle and circle at their exercise.

And Quasimodo's bird's-eye view
of big wigs and their retinue,
a five car Rolls Royce motorcade
of judgement draped in Town Hall braid,
I've watched the golden maces sweep
from courtrooms to the Castle keep
through winding Durham, the elect
before whom ids must genuflect.

But some stay standing and at one
God's irritating carrillon
brings you to me; I feel like the hunch-
back taking you for lunch;

then bed. All afternoon two church-
high prison helicopters search
for escapees down by the Wear
and seem as though they're coming here.

Listen! Their choppers guillotine
all the enemies there've ever been
of Church and State, including me
for taking this small liberty.
Liberal, lover, communist,
Czechoslovakia, Cuba, grist,
grist for the power-driven mill
weltering in overkill.

And England? Quiet Durham? Threat
smokes off our lives like steam off wet
subsidences when summer rain
drenches the workings. You complain
that the machinery of sudden death,
Fascism, the hot bad breath
of Powers down small countries' necks
shouldn't interfere with sex.

They *are* sex, love, we must include
all these in love's beatitude.
Bad weather and the public mess
drive us to private tenderness,
though I wonder if together we,
alone two hours, can ever be
love's anti-bodies in the sick,
sick body politic.

At best we're medieval masons, skilled
but anonymous within our guild,
at worst defendants hooded in a car
charged with something sinister.
On the *status quo*'s huge edifice
we're just excrescences that kiss,
cathedral gargoyles that obtrude
their acts of 'moral turpitude'.

But turpitude still keeps me warm
in foul weather as I head for home
down New Elvet, through the town,
past the butcher closing down,
hearing the belfry jumble time
out over Durham. As I climb
rain blankets the pithills, mist
the chalkings of the anarchist.

I wait for the six-five Plymouth train
glowering at Durham. First rain,
then hail, like teeth spit from a skull,
then fog obliterate it. As we pull
out of the station through the dusk and fog,
there, lighting up, is Durham, dog
chasing its own cropped tail,
University, Cathedral, Gaol.

Ghosts: Some Words Before Breakfast

for Jane

'These rooms have been furnished by the League of Friends
For your comfort and rest while illness portends.
Take care of the things which from us you borrow
For others are certain to need them tomorrow.'
(Inscribed in the League of Friends rest room, Royal Victoria Infirmary,
Newcastle-upon-Tyne)

'*C'est mon unique soutien au monde, à présent!*'
(Arthur Rimbaud, 2 July 1891, *Oeuvres*, p. 528)

A *Scottish & Newcastle* clops
past the RVI and traffic stops
to let the anachronistic dray
turn right into the brewery.
Victoria, now that daylight's gone,
whitens, and a Park lake swan
loops its pliant neck to scoff
the bits of sandwich floating off
the boathouse jetty. Empress, Queen,
here slender, beddable, your clean-
living family image drove
my mother venomously anti love,
and made her think the stillbirth just
retribution for our filthy lust;
our first (the one we married for)
red splashes on a LADIES floor . . .
inter urinam et faeces nasc-
imur . . . issues of blood. You ask,
as brought to bed you blench and bleed,
then scream, insisting that I read,
as blood comes out in spurts like piss,
a bit of *Pride & Prejudice*.

I will her breaths. Again! Again!
my daughter heaves in oxygen
and lives, each heaved breath
another lurch away from death,
each exhalation like death throes,
a posser squelched down on wet clothes,
and the only sign of life I see
is a spitting tracheotomy.
When you're conscious, Jane, we'll read
how that caparisoned, white steed
helped the younger son get past
leafage clinging like *Elastoplast*
and win through to bestow the kiss
that works the metamorphosis.
But frogs stay frogs, the briar grows
thicker and thicker round the rose.
I stoop to kiss away your pain
through stuff like florist's cellophane,
but my kiss can't make you less
the helpless prey of Nothingness –
ring-a-ring-a-roses . . . love
goes gravewards but does move.
Love's not something you can hoard
against the geriatric ward.
Mother, all, *all*, of us in this
brave trophallaxis of a kiss
that short-circuits generations scent
mortality's rich nutriment.

The waiting room's an airless place
littered with comics: *Spectre*; *Space*;
Adventure; love and hate
in AD 3068:
interplanetary affairs
policed by *Superlegionaires*:
STONE BOY of the planet Zwen
who turns to stone and back again,
and BRAINIAC, space-genius,

who finds Earth's labs ridiculous,
and MATTER-EATER-LAD resist
the mad, moon-exiled scientist –
Dr MANTIS MORLO! Will he smash
our heroes into lunar ash?
Air! Air! There's not enough
air in this small world. I'll suf-
focate. Air! Air! – In each black
PVC disposal sack,
I see two of my dimensions gone
into a flat oblivion.
Weightless, like a stranger caught
loosely flapping on my mother's grate,
down corridors, a shadow man,
I almost sleepwalk, float past *An-
aesthesia*, *X-Ray*, *Speech
Therapy* and, come full circle, reach
again the apparatus where you lie
between the armless and the eyeless boy.
I sicken. Jane! I could cut off
your breathing with a last wet cough,
break the connections, save you from
almost a lifetime's crippledom,
legs splayed outwards, the crushed bones
like the godfish Olokun's.

The black spot crossing; on both sides
a blank male silhouette still strides
off the caution and just keeps
on striding, while Newcastle sleeps,
between the Deaf School and the Park,
into his element, the dark.
The Scottish drivers have begun
the last stretch of the homeward run;
another hundred and they'll pull
into the brightening capital,
each lashed, tarpaulined hulk
groaning borderwards: *Blue Circle Bulk*

Cement; *Bulk Earthmoving*; *Bulk Grain*;
Edinburgh and back again.
And up the Great North Road in twos
great tankers of Newcastle booze,
returning empty, leaving full,
swashing with comfort for John Bull
and John Bull's bouncing babes who slug
their English anguish at the bottle's dug.
O caravanserais! I too could drown
this newest sorrow in *Newcastle Brown*.
I thrash round desperately. I flail
my arms at sharks in seas of ale.
Organs. Head/-lights/-lines. Black. White.
The on/off sirening blue light;
heart/lungs like a grappled squid;
BLIND PARAPLEGIC'S CHANNEL BID.
Blood; piss; oceans; taste of salt.
Halt! Halt! Halt! Halt!

I surface and the Tynemouth Queen,
that death's door study streaked with green,
is sitting dwarfish, slumped, alone
on her seawind-eroded throne,
scowling at a glimpse of sea
and wrecked, Dane-harried priory.
Above the grounded RVI
a few wind-driven seagulls cry
like grizzling kids. Out there; out there
where everything is sea and air,
at Tynemouth and at Seaton Sluice,
the sea works bits of England loose,
and redeposits on the land
the concrete tanktraps as blown sand.
Blood transfusion, saline drip,
'this fiddle' and 'stiff upper lip'
have seen us so far.

      You'll live,
like your father, a contemplative.

Daylight, but a pale *Blue Star*
still just glimmers on the nearest bar.
An orderly brings tea and toast.
Mother, wife and daughter, ghost –
I've laid, laid, laid, laid
you, but I'm still afraid,
though now Newcastle's washed with light,
about the next descent of night.

I

Think of your conception, you'll soon forget
what Plato puffs you up with, all that
'immortality' and 'divine life' stuff.

*Man, why dost thou think of Heaven? Nay
consider thine origins in common clay*

's one way of putting it but not blunt enough.

Think of your father, sweating, drooling, drunk,
you, his spark of lust, his spurt of spunk.

2

Ignorant of all logic and all law
Fortune follows her own blind course,
kind to the criminal, trampling on the just,
flaunting her irrational, brute force.

3

Life's a performance. Either join in
lightheartedly, or thole the pain.

4

Born naked. Buried naked. So why fuss?
All life leads to that first nakedness.

5

Born crying, and after crying, die.
It seems the life of man's just one long cry.

77

Pitiful and weak and full of tears,
Man shows his face on earth and disappears.

6

Our nostrils snuffle life from delicate air.
We turn our faces to the sun's bright glare,
organs that get their life out of a breeze.
Give our windpipes just one stiffish squeeze,
life's gone, we're brought down low to death.

We're puff and bluster cut off with one press,
utter nothings, sustained by nothingness
browsing the thin air for our life-breath.

7

Why this desperation to move heaven and earth
to try to change what's doled out at your birth,
the lot you're made a slave to by the gods?

Learn to love tranquillity, and against all odds
coax your glum spirit to its share of mirth.

8

Man's clay, and such a measly bit
and measuring the Infinite!

Leave geography alone, you can't survey
the paltry area of that poor clay.

Forget the spheres and first assess
not space but your own littleness.

9

Agony comes from brooding about death.
        Once dead, a man's spared all that pain.

Weeping for the dead's a waste of breath –
        they're lucky, *they* can't die again.

10

If gale-force Fortune sweeps you off your feet,
    let it; ride it; and admit defeat.

There's no point in resisting; it's too strong –
    willy-nilly, you'll get swept along.

11

Death's a debt that everybody owes,
and if you'll last the night out no one knows.

Learn your lesson then, and thank your stars
for wine and company and all-night bars.

Life careers gravewards at a breakneck rate,
so drink and love, and leave the rest to Fate.

12

Don't fash yourself, man! Don't complain.
Compared with those dark vastnesses before
and after, life's too brief to be a bore
and you'll never pass this way again.

So until the day you're in your grave
and inevitably you become an incubator
for the new-born worms, don't you behave
as though damned here and now, as well as later.

13

Each new daybreak we are born again.

All our life till now has flown away.

What we did yesterday's already gone.

All we have left of life begins today.

Old men, don't complain of all your years.
Those that have vanished are no longer yours!

14

Life's an ocean-crossing where winds howl
and the wild sea comes at us wave after wave.

With Fortune our pilot, weather fair or foul,
all alike drop anchor in the grave.

15

God's philosophical and so can wait
for the blasphemer and the reprobate —

He calmly chalks their crimes up on His slate.

16

God rot the guts and the guts' indulgences.
It's their fault that sobriety lets go.

17

Observe decorum in your grief. First drink and eat.
Remember Homer's:

> *Guts grieve for nothing but more food.*

Remember his Niobe, burying her butchered brood,
all twelve children, with her mind on meat.

18

Death feeds us up, keeps an eye on our weight
and herds us like pigs through the abattoir gate.

19

Loving the rituals that keep men close,
Nature created means for friends apart:

pen, paper, ink, the alphabet,
signs for the distant and disconsolate heart.

20

Hope! Fortune! *Je m'en fous!*
Both cheats, but I've come through.

Penniless but free, I can ignore
wealth that looks down on the poor.

21

Shun the rich, they're shameless sods
strutting about like little gods,

loathing poverty, the soul
of temperance and self-control.

22

When you start sneering it's not me
you're sneering at, it's poverty.

If he'd been poor and human, Zeus
'd've suffered from the same abuse.

23

Yes, I'm poor. What's wrong with that?
What is it that I've done to earn your hate?

It's not my character you're sneering at,
only the usual senselessness of Fate.

24

Just look at them, the shameless well-to-do
and stop feeling sorry you're without a sou.

25

It's no great step for a poor man to the grave.
    He's lived his life out only half-alive.

But when the man of plenty nears the end of his,
    Death yawns beneath him like a precipice.

26

So, Mister Moneybags, you're loaded? So?
You'll never take it with you when you go.

You've made your pile, but squandered time. Grown old
you can't gloat over age like hoarded gold.

27

Totting up the takings, quick Death can
reckon much faster than the businessman,

who, balancing, blacks out for ever, still
with the total ringing on the till.

28

Racing, reckoning fingers flick
at the abacus. Death's double-quick
comptometer works out the sums.

The stiffening digits, the rigid thumbs
still the clicking. Each bead slides
like a soul passing over, to the debit side.

29

Poor devil that I am, being so attacked
by wrath in fiction, wrath in fact.

Victim of wrath in literature and life:

1. The *Iliad* and 2. the wife!

30

Grammar commences with a 5-line curse:
Wrath's first and *fatal*'s second verse;

then *sufferings*. The third verse sends
many men to various and violent ends,
and then the fourth and fifth expose
men to Zeus's anger, dogs and crows.

Sad study, grammar! Its whole content's
one long string of accidents!

31

It's grammarians that the gods torment
and Homer's *fatal wrath*'s their instrument.

Monthly (if that!) the grudging nanny wraps
their measly pittance in papyrus scraps.
She nicks some, switches coins, and not content
holds out her grasping claws for 10%,
then lays at teacher's feet a screw of stuff
like paper poppies on a cenotaph.

Just get one loving father to agree
to pay (in decent gold!) a *yearly* fee,
the eleventh month, just when it's almost due,
he'll hire a 'better teacher' and fire you.

Your food and lodging gone, he's got the gall
to crack after-dinner jokes about it all.

32

Nouns *and* poor grammarians decline.
I'm selling off these rotten books of mine,
my Pindar, my Callimachus, the lot.
I'm a bad 'case'. It's poverty I've got.
Dorotheus has given me the sack
and slanders me behind my back.

Help me, Theon, or all that'll stand
between poverty and me's an &

33

Poor little donkey! It's no joke
being a pedant's not a rich man's moke
preened in the palace of the alabarch.

Exist on all the *carets* that I mark
in pupils' proses, little donkey, stay
with me patiently until the day
I get my (patience's first morpheme) pay.

34

This is my mule, a poor long-suffering hack
    with iambic front legs and trochaic back.

Backwards or forwards, he'll take you home
    both ways together like a palindrome.

35

I need mulled wine. Mull? Mull?
O your etymology's a load of bull!

I don't care if it is the Hebrides,
all I need is more mulled vino, *please*.

Old Norse, Gaelic or Teutonic,
it's still a first-rate stomach tonic.

You fetch the lexicon. Mull! Schmull!
Stuff etymology, when my cup's full.

36

A grammarian's daughter had a man
then bore a child m. f. & n.

37

You brainless bastard! O you stupid runt!
Such showing off and you so ignorant!
When the talk's linguistics, you look bored;

your specialism's Plato. Bloody fraud!
Someone says 'Ah, Plato!' then you duck
behind some weighty new phonetics book.

Linguistics! Plato Studies! Dodge and switch,
you haven't a clue, though, which is which.

38

The ignorant man does well to shut his trap
and hide his opinions like a dose of clap.

39

Menander's right, and thought's most fertile soil
　's serendipity, not midnight oil.

40

A lifetime's teaching grammar come to this –
　returned as member for Necropolis!

41. *On Gessius*

I

Fate didn't hustle Gessius to his death.
He ran there well before it, out of breath.

II

A mortal's better off not deified
or arrogantly over-elevated.

Look at Gessius, always dissatisfied,
puffed up first, and then deflated.

III

Two crystal-gazers gazed and prophesied
a consulate for Gessius. There wasn't and he died.

Mankind, self-destructive, puffed up with vanities,
even Death itself can't put you wise.

IV

Neglect of *Nothing in excess*
landed Gessius in this pretty mess.
Erudite he may be but a loon
thinking he could reach the moon.
Bellerophon spurred his mount too far
to learn what heavenly bodies are;
he had youth and strength, and he was on
winged Pegasus, was Bellerophon.

Gessius has nothing. Poor Gessius, I fear
hasn't the energy for diarrhoea!

42. *Maurus*

The politician's elephantine conk's
amazing, amazing too the voice that honks
through blubber lips (1 lb. net each)
spouting his loud, ear-shattering speech.

43

Where's the public good in what you write,
raking it in from all that shameless shite,

hawking iambics like so much *Betterbrite*?

44

Better the hangman's noose than surgeon's knife.
The executioner takes life for life
in legalized hatred for those who kill –

the surgeon does you in and sends a bill!

45

There's that old saying: *Ex-domestics can't
run houses of their own.* My equivalent

's: *An advocate's no judge* though he's
as great a pleader as Isocrates.

Those who sell eloquence like common whores
'll foul pure Justice with their dirty paws.

46

𝕸𝖊𝖎𝖓 𝕭𝖗𝖊𝖆𝖘𝖙, 𝖒𝖊𝖎𝖓 𝕮𝖔𝖗𝖘𝖊𝖙 𝖚𝖓𝖉 𝖒𝖊𝖎𝖓 𝕷𝖊𝖌𝖘
𝕴𝖆 𝖉𝖊𝖉𝖎𝖈𝖆𝖙𝖊𝖘 𝖙𝖔 𝕵𝖚𝖎𝖈𝖊 𝖑𝖎𝖐𝖊 𝖆𝖑𝖑 𝖌𝖚𝖙 𝕲𝖗𝖎𝖊𝖌𝖘.

47

I was promised a horse but what I got instead
was a tail, with a horse hung from it almost dead.

48

Thanks for the haggis. Could you really spare
such a huge bladder so full of air?

49

When you send out invitations, don't ask me.
It's rare fillets that I like not filigree.
A piece of pumpkin each! The table creaks
not with the weight of food but your antiques.

Save your *soirées* for connoisseurs who'll notch
their belts in tighter for a chance to watch
the long procession of your silverware,
for art's sake happy just to starve and stare,
and, for some fine piece to goggle at, forgo
all hope of eating, if the hallmarks show.

50

You invite me out, but if I can't attend
I've had the honour and I'm more your friend.

The heart's no gourmet, no it feels
honour stays hunger more than meals.

51

women all
cause rue

but can be nice
on   occasional

moments two
to be precise

in   bed

& dead

52

Cuckolded husbands have no certain sign
that trusted wives are treacherous, *like mine*.
The ugly woman's not *de facto* pure,
nor every beauty fast. You're never sure.
The beddable girl, though every bidder woos
with cash and comfort's likely to refuse.
There's many a plain nympho who bestows
expensive gifts on all her gigolos.

The serious woman, seemingly man-shy
and never smiling, does that mean chastity?
Such gravity's worn only out of doors;
at home, in secret, they're all utter whores.
The chatty woman with a word for all
may well be chaste, though that's improbable.
Even old age gets goaded into lust;
senility's no guarantee. What can we trust?

I've got twelve gods to swear my honour by,
she, convenient Christianity!

53

The theft of fire. Man's worst bargain yet.
Zeus created Woman, He was that upset!

A woman desiccates a man with cares
and soon gives golden youth his first grey hairs.

But Zeus's married life in Heaven above
's no cloudy mattress of ambrosial love.

Zeus with Hera of the golden throne
longs to be divorced and on His own.

He often has to shove Her from the sky
to a dog-house cumulus to sulk and cry.

Homer knew this well and shows the two
squabbling on Olympus as mere mortals do.

Thus a woman nags and haggles though she lies
beside the Deity of Deities.

54

Man stole fire, and Zeus created flame
much fiercer still. Woman was its name.

Fire's soon put out, but women blaze
like volcanic conflagrations all our days.

55

The women all shout after me and mock:
Look in the mirror, you decrepit wreck!
But I'm too near the end to give a toss
for trivia like grey temples and hair-loss.

A nice, fresh deodorant, some after-shave
for banishing the bad smell of the grave,

a few bright flowers in my falling hair,
a good night's drinking, and I just don't care.

56

When he comes up to the bedroom
and switches on the light,
the poor man with the ugly wife
stares out into the night.

57

Zeus isn't such a raving Casanova
if he's seen this girl and passed her over.

No galloping bull or strong-winged giant swan
to get his hands on this proud courtesan,

who's Leda, Europa, Danaë all rolled
into one, worth ten showers of his gold.

Are courtesans too common to seduce
and only royal virgins fit for Zeus?

58

From Alexandria to Antioch.
From Syria to Italy: no luck!

Between the Tiber and the Nile
not one man to lead you up the aisle.

'Hope springs eternal . . .' though. Good luck, my dear,
husband-hunting through the Gazetteer.

59

With a son called Eros and a wife whose name
's Aphrodite, no wonder that you're lame!

60

Mere ants and gnats and trivia with stings

vent their aggression like all living things,
but you, you think that *I* ought to be meek,
lay myself open, 'turn the other cheek',
not even verbal comebacks, but stay dumb
and choking on my gag till Kingdom Come!

61

Boast you don't obey the wife, I'll say that's balls.
You're a man aren't you, and not a rock or log?
You suffer too. You know what bugs us all 's
being the husband and the underdog.

But say: *She doesn't slipper me or sleep around;*
no turning a blind eye, then, *if* that's true,
your bondage isn't bad, being only bound
to one who's chaste and not *too* hard on you.

62

A drink to drown my sorrows and restart
    the circulation to my frozen heart!

63. *On a Temple of Fortune turned into a tavern*

I
Agh, the world's gone all to fuck
when Luck herself's run out of luck!

II
Fortune, fortune maker/breaker,
human nature cocktail-shaker,

goddess once, and now a barmaid
's not too drastic change of trade!

You'll do nicely where you are
behind the counter of *The Fortune Bar*,

metamorphosed to 'mine host'
the character that suits you most.

III

Fortune, can you hear them making fun,
all the mortals, now you're one?

This time you've really gone too far
blotting out your own bright star.

Once queen of a temple, now you're old
you serve hot toddies to keep out the cold.

Well might you complain, now even you
suffer from yourself as mere men do.

64

The blacksmith's quite a logical man
to melt an Eros down and turn
the God of Love into a frying pan,
something that can also burn.

65

Knocked off his pedestal! THEY've
done *this* to Heracles?
Flabbergasted I began to rave
and went down on my knees:

Giant, whose birth took three whole days,
whose image stands at each crossroad,
you to whom the whole world prays,
our Champion, KOed?

That night he stood at my bed-end
and smiled and said: *I can't complain.*
The winds of change are blowing, friend,
your god's a weather-vane.

66. *Marina's House*

'Baptized' Olympians live here in peace,
spared Treasury furnace and coiner's mould,
the fires of revolution and small change.

67. *Hypatia*

Searching the zodiac, gazing on Virgo,
knowing your province is really the heavens,
finding your brilliance everywhere I look,
I render you homage, revered Hypatia,
teaching's bright star, unblemished, undimmed.

68. *On Monks*

Solitaries? I wonder whether
real solitaries live together?

Crowds of recluses? Pseuds,
pooling all their 'solitudes'.

69. *The Spartan Mother*

A Spartan lad fled from the war.
He didn't want no bullet.
He isn't home two ticks before
his mam's dagger's at his gullet.

She prods him with her stiletto blade
and pricks his yeller belly:
What, a son of mine afraid?
yer spineless little jelly.

If you're allowed to stay alive,
you miserable little crumb,
think how your rotten coward's skive
brings shame on your old mum.

That's if you don't die. If you do
'A mum's a proper martyr'
's what they'll say, but (she ran him through)
no shame for me or Sparta.

70. *The Murderer & Sarapis*

A murderer spread his palliasse
beneath a rotten wall

and in his dream came Sarapis
and warned him it would fall:

Jump for your life, wretch, and be quick!
One more second and you're dead.
He jumped and tons of crumbling brick
came crashing on his bed.

The murderer gasped with relief,
he thanked the gods above.
It was his innocent belief
they'd saved him out of love.

But once again came Sarapis
in the middle of the night,
and once more uttered prophecies
that set the matter right:

Don't think the gods have let you go
and connive at homicide.
We've spared you that quick crushing, so
we can get you crucified.

¶

Sentences

1. *Brazil*

Even the lone man
in his wattle lean-to,
the half-mad women
in their hive of leaves,
pitched at the roadside
by a low shared fire
so near the shoulder
that their tethered goat
crops only half-circles
of tough, scorched turf,
and occasional tremors
shake ash from the charcoal,
live for something more
than the manioc and curds
they're preparing,
barely attentive to speech
as they strain
through the oppressive mid-day drowse,
or, at night, through the noise
of the insects drilling into them
the lessons of loneliness
or failed pioneering
over miles of savannah,
for the punctual Bahia-Rio
coaches as they come
to the village of Milagres
they are outcasts from
for a quick *cafezinho*,
a quick piss,
edible necklaces
and caged red birds.

2. *Fonte Luminosa*

Walking on the Great North Road
with my back towards London
through showers of watery sleet,
my cracked rubber boot soles
croak like African bullfrogs
and the buses and lorries that swish
like a whiplash laid on and on
without intermission or backswing
send a spray splashing over
from squelching tyres skywards
STOP red, GO green, CAUTION
amber, and at the crossing
where you had your legs crushed
I remember the *fonte luminosa*,
Brasilia's musical geyser
spurting a polychrome plumage,
the fans of rich pashas,
a dancer's dyed ostriches,
making parked Chevrolets
glisten, people seem sweaty,
and when yellowing, loppy Terezinha,
the eldest, though your age,
of the children all huddled
under the fancy ramp entrance
of the National Theatre,
comes and scoops from the churned
illuminated waters a tinful
for drinking and cooking and goes
gingerly to ingenious roads
where cars need never once
stop at Belishas or crossings,
intersect, crash, or slow down,
the drops that she scatters
are not still orange or purple,
still greenish or gorgeous
in any way, or still gushing,

but slightly clouded like quartz,
and at once they're sucked back
into Brazil like a whelk
retracting, like the tear
that drains back into your eye
as once more you start coming through
the rainbowing spindrift and fountains
of your seventh anaesthesia.

3. *Isla de la Juventud*

The fireflies that women
once fattened on sugar
and wore in their hair
or under the see-through
parts of their blouses
in Cuba's *Oriente*,
here seem to carry
through the beam where they cluster
a brief phosphorescence
from each stiff corpse
on the battlefields that look
like the blown-up towel
of a careless barber,
its nap and its bloodflecks,
and if you were to follow,
at Santa Fe's open-air
cinema's Russian
version *War & Peace*,
the line of the dead
to the end, corpses,
cannons and fetlocks,
scuffing the red crust
with your snowboots,
or butt-end of your rifle,
you would enter an air
as warm as the blankets
just left by a lover,
yours, if you have one,
an air full of fireflies,
bright after-images,
and scuffed Krasnoe snow
like unmeltable stars.

4. *On the Spot*

for Miroslav Holub,
Havana, August 1969

Watching the Soviet subs surface
at the side of flagged battleships
between Havana harbour and the USA
I can't help thinking how the sword
has developed immensely,
how only nomads in deserts
still lop heads off with it,
while the pen is still only
a point, a free ink-flow
and the witness it has to keep bearing.

Miroslav, you must remember
there'd be no rumba now,
if the blacks who made Cuba
had not somehow evolved
either when shackled or pegged
or grouped for a whiplash harangue
or under the driver's bluebottle eye
following their own eyes flicking,
flies dying in jam-jars
jerking all over –

　　Think
of those trapped pupils let loose,
the offal they'd flock to,
O have to, being so hungry,
History inescapable, high,
necessary, putrescent,
unburied, still not picked over,
only the balls of it gnawed at –

had not evolved as I said,
together, somehow, with slight spasms
of only the nipples or haunches,

a calf-muscle tugging the chain taut,
the art of dancing on the spot
without ever being seen to be moving,
not a foot or a hand out of place.

Voortrekker

A spoor from a kraal. Then grass
greens the turd of the carnivore
gone all gums. So the sick Boer
lays on with the whip less.

Panic in him and round him
like a wind-flapped tilt –
only the sable sons of Ham
cram Death's dark veld.

Coupled together in God's span,
outnumbered many times over,
ox, dog, Hottentot, Caffre,
and just one Christian man.

The Bonebard Ballads

1. *The Ballad of Babelabour*

'This Babylonian confusion of words results from
their being the language of men who are going down.
(Bertolt Brecht)

What ur-𝕾𝖕𝖗𝖆𝖈𝖍𝖊 did the labour speak?
ur ur ur to t'master's 𝕾𝖕𝖗𝖆𝖈𝖍𝖊
the hang-cur ur-grunt of the weak
the unrecorded urs of gobless workers

Their snaptins kept among their turds
they labour   eat and shit
with only grunts not proper words
raw material for t'poet

They're their own meat and their own dough
another block   another
a palace for the great Pharaoh
a prison for their brothers

Whatever name's carved on those stones
it's not the one who labours
an edifice of workers' bones
for one who wants no neighbours

Nimrod's nabobs like their bards
to laud the state's achievements
to eulogize his house of cards
and mourn the king's bereavements

The treasurer of 𝕾𝖕𝖗𝖆𝖈𝖍𝖊's court
drops the bard his coppers
He knows that poets aren't his sort
but belong to the ur-crappers

Ur-crappers tongueless bardless nerks
your condition's shitty
no time for yer Collected Works
or modulated pity

but ur ur ur ur ur ur urs
sharpened into 𝔖prache
revurlooshunairy vurse
uprising nacker starkers

by the time the bards have urd
and urd and urd and 𝔖prachered
the world's all been turned into *merde*
& Nimrod's Noah'sarkered

sailing t'shit in t'ship they urd at
no labour can embark her
try and you'll get guard-dog grrred at
the shitship's one class: 𝔖prache

Bards & labour left for dead
the siltworld's neue neue
bard   the HMV doghead
in that *negra negra* Goya.

(See the picture 'A Dog Buried in the Sand'
among the Black Paintings of Goya in the Prado.)

2. *The Ballad of the Geldshark*

(from Aeschylus)

Geldshark Ares god of War
broker of men's bodies
usurer of living flesh
corpse-trafficker that god is –

give to War your men's fleshgold
and what are your returns?
kilos of cold clinker packed
in army-issue urns

wives   mothers   sisters each one scans
the dogtags on the amphorae
which grey ashes are my man's
they sift the jumbled names and cry:

My husband sacrificed his life
My brother battle-martyr
Aye   for someone else's wife
Helen   whore of Sparta

whisper   mutter   belly-aching
the people's beef and bile: *This war's*
been the clanchiefs' making
the ruling clanchiefs' so-called 'cause'.

Where's my father   husband   boy?
where do all our loved ones lie?

six feet under near the Troy
they died to occupy.

3. 'Flying down to Rio':

A Ballad of Beverly Hills

Big mouth of the horn of plenty
horny   horny Hollywood
Food   flesh   fashion *cognoscenti*
grudge the midge her mite of blood

Fat bugs fry and small gnats ping
against *Insectecutor* bars
so no slight unsightly sting
blemishes the flesh of stars

Don't adjust the skew-whiff Manet
you'll touch off the thief device
monitored each nook and cranny
of this closed circuit paradise

but tonight she's feeling spooky
plucking plasmic plectra strike her
nervestrings like a bop bazouki
boogie-woogie balalaika

Divinely draped in 3rd World 'folk art'
(Locations where the labour's cheap!)
unaware she'll soon join Bogart
big C first and then big sleep

Brown tits $\frac{7}{8}$ on show'll
scotch the lies they're not her own
Death's the only gigolo 'll
rumble that they're silicone

Death   the riveting romancer
in sheerest X-ray underwear
nimble-footed fancy dancer
bonier than Fred Astaire

Girning atcha *gotcha gotcha*
(on his dance card once you're born)

cold carioca or chill cha-cha
charnelwise to Forest Lawn

Or choker sheikh whose robes hang loose
O worse than loss of honour fate!
His kisser sags from black burnous
your veils are blue barbiturate

Freeway skiddy with crashed star's gore
(fastlivingwecanshow'em!)
the jelling jugular 'll pour
at least a jereboam . . .

Places that you once changed planes at
or hardened second units shot
this afterlife eternal flat
horizonless back lot

places   faces from your worst dream
say   starvelings of Recife
who made your slimmer's body seem
embarrassingly beefy

On such locations old at twenty
boys grub green crabs from grey mud –
big mouth of the horn of plenty
horny   horny Hollywood.

Social Mobility

Ah, the proved advantages of scholarship!
Whereas his dad took cold tea for his snap,
he slaves at nuances, knows at just one sip
Château Lafite *from* Château Neuf du Pape.

from
THE SCHOOL OF ELOQUENCE

'In 1799 special legislation was introduced "utterly suppressing and prohibiting" by name the London Corresponding Society and the United Englishmen. Even the indefatigable conspirator, John Binns, felt that further national organization was hopeless . . . When arrested he was found in possession of a ticket which was perhaps one of the last "covers" for the old LCS: *Admit for the Season to the School of Eloquence.*'

(E. P. Thompson, *The Making of the English Working Class*)

Nunc mea Pierios cupiam per pectora fontes
Irriguas torquere vias, totumque per ora
Volvere laxatum gemino de vertice rivum;
Ut, tenues oblita sonos, audacibus alis
Surgat in officium venerandi Musa parentis.
Hoc utcunque tibi gratum, pater optime, carmen
Exiguum meditatur opus, nec novimus ipsi
Aptius a nobis quae possint munera donis
Respondere tuis, quamvis nec maxima possint
Respondere tuis, nedum ut par gratia donis
Esse queat, vacuis quae redditur arida verbis . . .

Si modo perpetuos sperare audebitis annos,
Et domini superesse rogo, lucemque tueri,
Nec spisso rapient oblivia nigra sub Orco,
Forsitan has laudes, decantatumque parentis
Nomen, ad exemplum, servo servabitis aevo.

(John Milton, 1637)

Heredity

How you became a poet's a mystery!
Wherever did you get your talent from?
I say: I had two uncles, Joe and Harry –
one was a stammerer, the other dumb.

ONE **On Not Being Milton**

for Sergio Vieira & Armando Guebuza (Frelimo)

Read and committed to the flames, I call
these sixteen lines that go back to my roots
my *Cahier d'un retour au pays natal*,
my growing black enough to fit my boots.

The stutter of the scold out of the branks
of condescension, class and counter-class
thickens with glottals to a lumpen mass
of Ludding morphemes closing up their ranks.
Each swung cast-iron Enoch of Leeds stress
clangs a forged music on the frames of Art,
the looms of owned language smashed apart!

Three cheers for mute ingloriousness!

Articulation is the tongue-tied's fighting.
In the silence round all poetry we quote
Tidd the Cato Street conspirator who wrote:

Sir, I Ham a very Bad Hand at Righting.

Note. An 'Enoch' is an iron sledge-hammer used by the Luddites to smash the frames which were also made by the same Enoch Taylor of Marsden. The cry was: 'Enoch made them, Enoch shall break them!'

The Rhubarbarians

I

Those glottals glugged like poured pop, each
rebarbative syllable, remembrancer, raise
'mob' *rhubarb-rhubarb* to a tribune's speech
crossing the crackle as the hayricks blaze.

The gaffers' blackleg Boswells at their side.
Horsfall of Ottiwells, if the bugger could,
'd've liked to (exact words recorded) *ride
up to my saddle-girths in Luddite blood*.

What t'mob said to the cannons on the mills,
shouted to soldier, scab and sentinel
's silence, parries and hush on whistling hills,
shadows in moonlight playing knurr and spell.

It wasn't poetry though. Nay, wiseowl Leeds
pro rege et lege schools, nobody needs
your drills and chanting to parrot right
the *tusky-tusky* of the pikes that night.

II

(On translating Smetana's *Prodaná Nevěsta* for the
Metropolitan Opera, New York.)

One afternoon the Band Conductor up on his stand
Somehow lost his baton it flew out of his hand
So I jumped in his place and conducted the band
With mi little stick of Blackpool Rock!
George Formby

Finale of ACT II. Though I resist
blurring the clarity of *hanba* (shame)
not wanting the least nuance to be missed
syllables run to rhubarb just the same . . .

Sorry, dad, you won't get that quatrain
(I'd like to be the poet my father reads!)
It's all from you once saying on the train
how most of England's rhubarb came from Leeds.

Crotchets and quavers, rhubarb silhouettes,
dark-shy sea-horse heads through waves of dung!
Rhubarb arias, duets, quartets
soar to precision from our common tongue.

The uke in the attic manhole once was yours!

Watch me on the rostrum wave my arms –

mi little stick of Leeds grown *tusky* draws
galas of rhubarb from the MET-set palms.

Note. Tusky: the Leeds word for rhubarb.

Study

Best clock. Best carpet. Best three chairs.

For deaths, for Christmases, a houseless aunt,
for those too old or sick to manage stairs.

I try to whistle in it but I can't.

Uncle Joe came here to die. His gaping jaws
once plugged in to the power of his stammer
patterned the stuck plosive without pause
like a d-d-damascener's hammer.

Mi aunty's baby still. The dumbstruck mother.
The mirror, tortoise-shell-like celluloid
held to it, passed from one hand to another.
No babble, blubber, breath. The glass won't cloud.

The best clock's only wound for layings out
so the stillness isn't tapped at by its ticks.
The settee's shapeless underneath its shroud.

My mind moves upon silence and *Aeneid* VI.

Me Tarzan

Outside the whistled gang-call, *Twelfth Street Rag*,
then a Tarzan yodel for the kid who's bored,
whose hand's on his liana . . . no, back
to Labienus and his flaming sword.

Off laikin', then to t'fish 'oil all the boys,
off tartin', off to t'flicks but on, on, on,
the foldaway card table, the green baize,
De Bello Gallico and lexicon.

It's only his jaw muscles that he's tensed
into an enraged *shit* that he can't go;
down with polysyllables, he's against
all pale-face Caesars, *for* Geronimo.

He shoves the frosted attic skylight, shouts:

Ah bloody can't ah've gorra Latin prose.

His bodiless head that's poking out 's
like patriarchal Cissy-bleeding-ro's.

Wordlists

'There was only one more thing which had to be done, a last
message to leave behind on the last day of all: and so he gather-
ed up his strength in the midst of a long stretch of silence
and framed his lips to say to me quite clearly the one word
Dictionary.'

(The Life of Joseph Wright, 1858–1930)

I

Good parrots got good marks. I even got
a 100 in Divinity (posh schools' RI),
learned new long words and (wrongly stressed) *harlót*
I asked the meaning of so studiously.

I asked mi mam. She said she didn't know.
The Classics/RI master hummed and hawed.
(If only he'd've said it was a pro!)
New words: 'venery', 'VD' and 'bawd'!

Sometime . . . er . . . there's summat in that drawer . . .

photograph foetuses, a pinman with no prick,
things I learned out laiking years before
they serialized 'Life' in the *Sunday Pic*.

Words and wordlessness. Between the two
the gauge went almost ga-ga. No RI,
no polysyllables could see me through,
come glossolalia, dulciloquy.

II

The *Funk & Wagnalls*? Does that still survive?
Uncle Harry most eloquent deaf-mute
jabbed at its lexis till it leaped to life
when there were Tory errors to confute.

A bible paper bomb that dictionary.
I learned to rifle through it at great speed.
He's dead. I've studied, got the OED
and other tongues I've slaved to speak or read:

L & S dead Latin, L & S dead Greek,
one the now dead lexicographer gave me,
Ivan Poldauf, his English-Czech *slovník*;
Harrap's French 2 vols, a Swahili,
Cabrera's Afro-Cuban *Anagó*,
Hausa, Yoruba, both R.C. Abraham's –

but not the tongue that once I used to know
but can't bone up on now, and that's mi mam's.

III

The treasure found here on this freezing shore,
with last war tanktraps, and oil-clagged birds,
the morning shivery, the seawinds raw,
is the memory of a man collecting words.

Crushed scallops, washed up hard hats, shit, what fitter
thesaurus trove of trashes could he wish,
our lexicographer and *Doctor Litter-*
arum netting a fine but unexpected fish?

His heart beat faster when a living mouth
(the jotting said a 'fishwife's') used the old
and, for him forgotten in his flit down South,
border word *yagach* to describe the cold.

Though society 's not like the OED
and the future 's just as yagach as the day,
I celebrate beside the same bleak sea
James Murray, and a scholar's clarion call
that set those sharp speech combers on their way:

Fling our doors wide! all, all, not one, but all!

Classics Society

(Leeds Grammar School 1552–1952)

The grace of Tullies eloquence doth excell
any Englishmans tongue ... my barbarous stile ...

The tongue our leaders use to cast their spell
was once denounced as 'rude', 'gross', 'base' and 'vile'.

How fortunate we are who've come so far!

We boys can take old Hansards and translate
the British Empire into SPQR
but nothing demotic or too up-to-date,
and *not* the English that I speak at home,
not Hansard standards, and if Antoninus
spoke like delinquent Latin back in Rome
he'd probably get gamma double minus.

And so the lad who gets the alphas works
the hardest in his class at his translation
and finds good Ciceronian for Burke's:

a dreadful schism in the British nation.

National Trust

Bottomless pits. There's one in Castleton,
and stout upholders of our law and order
one day thought its depth worth wagering on
and borrowed a convict hush-hush from his warder
and winched him down; and back, flayed, grey, mad,
    dumb.

Not even a good flogging made him holler!

O gentlemen, a better way to plumb
the depths of Britain's dangling a scholar,
say, here at the booming shaft at Towanroath,
now National Trust, a place where they got tin,
those gentlemen who silenced the men's oath
and killed the language that they swore it in.

The dumb go down in history and disappear
and not one gentleman 's been brought to book:

Mes den hep tavas a-gollas y dyr

(Cornish) –
            'the tongueless man gets his land took.'

Them & [uz]

for Professors Richard Hoggart & Leon Cortez

I

αἰαῖ, ay, ay! . . . stutterer Demosthenes
gob full of pebbles outshouting seas –

4 words only of *mi 'art aches* and . . . 'Mine's broken,
you barbarian, T.W.!' *He* was nicely spoken.
'Can't have our glorious heritage done to death!'

I played the Drunken Porter in *Macbeth*.

'Poetry's the speech of kings. You're one of those
Shakespeare gives the comic bits to: prose!
All poetry (even Cockney Keats?) you see
's been dubbed by [ʌs] into RP,
Received Pronunciation, please believe [ʌs]
your speech is in the hands of the Receivers.'

'We say [ʌs] not [uz], T.W.!' That shut my trap.
I doffed my flat a's (as in 'flat cap')
my mouth all stuffed with glottals, great
lumps to hawk up and spit out . . . *E-nun-ci-ate*!

II

So right, yer buggers, then! We'll occupy
your lousy leasehold Poetry.

I chewed up Littererchewer and spat the bones
into the lap of dozing Daniel Jones,
dropped the initials I'd been harried as
and used my *name* and own voice: [uz] [uz] [uz],
ended sentences with by, with, from,
and spoke the language that I spoke at home.
RIP RP, RIP T.W.
I'm *Tony* Harrison no longer you!

You can tell the Receivers where to go
(and not aspirate it) once you know
Wordsworth's *matter/water* are full rhymes,
[uz] can be loving as well as funny.

My first mention in the *Times*
automatically made Tony Anthony!

Working

Among stooped getters, grimy, knacker-bare,
head down thrusting a 3 cwt corf
turned your crown bald, your golden hair
chafed fluffy first and then scuffed off,
chick's back, then eggshell, that sunless white.
You strike sparks and plenty but can't see.
You've been underneath too long to stand the light.
You're lost in this sonnet for the bourgeoisie.

Patience Kershaw, bald hurryer, fourteen,
this wordshift and inwit's a load of crap
for dumping on a slagheap, I mean
th'art nobbut summat as wants raking up.

I stare into the fire. Your skinned skull shines.
I close my eyes. That makes a dark like mines.

Wherever hardship held its tongue the job
's breaking the silence of the worked-out-gob.

Note. 'Gob': an old Northern coal-mining word for the space left after
the coal has been extracted. Also, of course, the mouth, and speech.

Cremation

So when she hears him clearing his throat
every few seconds she's aware what he's raking
's death off his mind; the next attack. The threat
of his dying has her own hands shaking.

The mangle brought it on. Taking it to bits.
She didn't need it now he'd done with pits.

A grip from behind that seems to mean *don't go*
tightens through bicep till the fingers touch.
His, his dad's and *his* dad's lifetime down below
crammed into one huge nightshift, and too much.

He keeps back death the way he keeps back phlegm
in company, curled on his tongue. Once left alone
with the last coal fire in the smokeless zone,
he hawks his cold gobful at the brightest flame,
too practised, too contemptuous to miss.

Behind the door she hears the hot coals hiss.

TWO   Book Ends

I

Baked the day she suddenly dropped dead
we chew it slowly that last apple pie.

Shocked into sleeplessness you're scared of bed.
We never could talk much, and now don't try.

You're like book ends, the pair of you, she'd say,
Hog that grate, say nothing, sit, sleep, stare . . .

The 'scholar' me, you, worn out on poor pay,
only our silence made us seem a pair.

Not as good for staring in, blue gas,
too regular each bud, each yellow spike.

A night you need my company to pass
and she not here to tell us we're alike!

Your life's all shattered into smithereens.

Back in our silences and sullen looks,
for all the Scotch we drink, what's still between 's
not the thirty or so years, but books, books, books.

II

The stone's too full. The wording must be terse.
There's scarcely room to carve the FLORENCE on it –

Come on, it's not as if we're wanting verse.
It's not as if we're wanting a whole sonnet!

After tumblers of neat *Johnny Walker*
(I think that both of us we're on our third)
you said you'd always been a clumsy talker
and couldn't find another, shorter word
for 'beloved' or for 'wife' in the inscription,
but not too clumsy that you can't still cut:

You're supposed to be the bright boy at description
and you can't tell them what the fuck to put!

I've got to find the right words on my own.

I've got the envelope that he'd been scrawling,
mis-spelt, mawkish, stylistically appalling
but I can't squeeze more love into their stone.

Confessional Poetry

for Jeffrey Wainwright

When Milton *sees* his 'late espoused saint'
are we sure the ghost's wife 1 or 2?
Does knowing it's himself beneath the paint
make the Rembrandts truer or less true?

But your father was a simple working man,
they'll say, *and didn't speak in those full rhymes.*
His words when *they came would scarcely scan.*

Mi dad's did scan, like yours do, many times!

That quarrel then in Book Ends II *between*
one you still go on addressing as 'mi dad'
and you, your father comes across as mean
but weren't the taunts you flung back just as bad?

We *had* a bitter quarrel in our cups
and there *were* words between us, yes,
I'm guilty, and the way I make it up 's
in poetry, and that much I confess.

Next Door

I

Ethel Jowett died still hoping not to miss
next year's *Mikado* by the D'Oyly Carte.
For being her 'male escort' (9!) to this
she gave my library its auspicious start:

The Kipling Treasury. My name. The date:
Tony Harrison   1946
in dip-in-penmanship type copperplate
with proper emphasis on thins and thicks.

Mi mam was 'that surprised' how many came
to see the cortège off and doff their hats –
All the 'old lot' left gave her the same
bussing back from 'Homes' and Old Folk's Flats.

Since mi mam dropped dead mi dad's took fright.

His dicky ticker beats its quick retreat:

It won't be long before Ah'm t'only white!

Or t'Town Hall's thick red line sweeps through t'whole
     street.

II

Their front garden (8 × 5) was one of those
the lazier could write off as 'la-di-dah'.
Her brother pipesmoked greenfly off each rose
in summer linen coat and Panama.

Hard-faced traders tore her rooms apart.
Litter and lavender in ransacked drawers,
the yearly programmes for the D'Oyly Carte.
'Three Little Maids' she'd marked with '4 encores!'

Encore! No more. A distant relative
roared up on a loud bike and poked around.
Mi mam cried when he'd gone, and spat out: *Spiv!*

I got Tennyson and Milton leather-bound.

The Sharpes came next. He beat her, blacked her eye.
Through walls I heard each blow, each *Cunt! Cunt! Cunt!*

The Jowetts' dahlias were left to die.

Now mi dad's the only one keeps up his front.

III

Also the only one who shifts his snow
and him long past his three score years and ten.

You *try* to understand: *Their sort don't know.*
They're from the sun. But wait till they're old men.

But if some from out that 'old lot' still survive
and, shopping for essentials, shuffle past,
they'll know by your three clear flags that you're alive
and, though you'll never speak, they're not the last.

Outside your clearing your goloshes slip.
The danger starts the moment you're next door –
the fall, the dreaded 'dislocated hip',
the body's final freeze-up with no thaw.

If you weren't scared you'd never use the phone!

The winter's got all England in its vice.

All night I hear a spade that scrapes on stone
and see our street one skidding slide of ice.

IV

All turbans round here now, forget flat caps!

They've taken over everything bar t'CO-OP.
Pork's gone west, chitt'lins, trotters, dripping baps!
And booze an' all, if it's a Moslem owns t'new shop.

Ay, t'Off Licence, that's gone Paki in t'same way!
(You took your jug and bought your bitter draught)
Ah can't get over it, mi dad'll say,
smelling curry in a pop shop. Seems all daft.

Next door but one this side 's front room wi t'
Singers *hell for leather all day long 's*
some sort o' sweatshop bi the looks on it
running up them dresses . . . them . . . sarongs!

Last of the 'old lot' still left in your block.
Those times, they're gone. The 'old lot' can't come back.

Both doors I notice now you double lock –

he's already in your shoes, your next-door black.

Long Distance

I

Your bed's got two wrong sides. Your life's all grouse.
I let your phone-call take its dismal course:

Ah can't stand it no more, this empty house!

Carrots choke us wi'out your mam's white sauce!

Them sweets you brought me, you can have 'em back.
Ah'm diabetic now. Got all the facts.
(The diabetes comes hard on the track
of two coronaries and cataracts.)

Ah've allus liked things sweet! But now ah push
food down mi throat! Ah'd sooner do wi'out.
And t'only reason now for beer 's to flush
(so t'dietician said) mi kidneys out.

When I come round, they'll be laid out, the sweets,
Lifesavers, my father's New World treats,
still in the big brown bag, and only bought
rushing through JFK as a last thought.

II

Though my mother was already two years dead
Dad kept her slippers warming by the gas,
put hot water bottles her side of the bed
and still went to renew her transport pass.

You couldn't just drop in. You had to phone.
He'd put you off an hour to give him time
to clear away her things and look alone
as though his still raw love were such a crime.

He couldn't risk my blight of disbelief
though sure that very soon he'd hear her key
scrape in the rusted lock and end his grief.
He *knew* she'd just popped out to get the tea.

I believe life ends with death, and that is all.
You haven't both gone shopping; just the same,
in my new black leather phone book there's your name
and the disconnected number I still call.

Flood

His home address was inked inside his cap
and on every piece of paper that he carried
even across the church porch of the snap
that showed him with mi mam just minutes married.

But if ah'm found at 'ome (he meant found dead)
turn t'water off. Through his last years he nursed,
more than a fear of dying, a deep dread
of his last bath running over, or a burst.

Each night towards the end he'd pull the flush
then wash, then in pyjamas, rain or snow,
go outside, kneel down in the yard, and push
the stopcock as far off as it would go.

For though hoping that he'd drop off in his sleep
he was most afraid, I think, of not being 'found'
there in their house, his ark, on firm Leeds ground
but somewhere that kept moving, cold, dark, deep.

The Queen's English

Last meal together, Leeds, the Queen's Hotel,
that grandish pile of swank in City Square.
Too posh for me! he said (though he dressed well)
If you weren't wi' me now ah'd nivver dare!

I knew that he'd decided that he'd die
not by the way he lingered in the bar,
nor by that look he'd give with one good eye,
nor the firmer handshake and the gruff *ta-ra*,
but when we browsed the station bookstall sales
he picked up *Poems from the Yorkshire Dales* –

*'ere tek this un wi' yer to New York
to remind yer 'ow us gaffers used to talk.
It's up your street in't it? ah'll buy yer that!*

The broken lines go through me speeding South –

As t'Doctor stopped to oppen woodland yat . . .
and
     wi' skill they putten wuds reet i' his mouth.

Aqua Mortis

Death's elixirs have their own golden gleam.
I see you clearly: one good, failing eye's
on morning piss caught clumsily 'midstream'
it's your first task of the day to analyse.

Each day dawns closer to the last *eureka*,
the urine phial held up to clouding rays
meaning all solutions in life's beaker
precipitate one night from all our days.

Alchemists keep skulls, and you have one
that stretches your skin taut and moulds your face,
and instead of a star sphere for sense of space
there's the transatlantic number of your son,
a 14-digit spell propped by the phone
whose girdling's giddy speed knocks spots off Puck's
but can't re-eye dry sockets or flesh bone.

My study is your skull. *I'll burn my books.*

Grey Matter

The ogling bottle cork with tasselled fez
bowing and scraping, rolling goo-goo eyes is
gippo King Farouk, whose lewd leer says:

I've had the lot, my lad, all shapes and sizes!

One night we kept him prancing and he poured,
filtered through his brains, his bulk of booze.
The whisky pantaloons sans sash or cord
swashed dad to the brink of twin taboos.
As King Farouk's eyes rolled, dad rolled his own:
That King Farouk! he said, and almost came
(though in the end it proved too near the bone)
to mentioning both sex and death by name.

I wake dad with what's left. King Leer's stare
stuck, though I shake him, and his fixed Sphinx smile
take in the ultimate a man can bear
and that dry Nothingness beyond the Nile.

An Old Score

Capless, conscious of the cold patch on my head
where my father's genes have made me almost bald
I walk along the street where he dropped dead,
my hair cut his length now, although I'm called
poet, in my passport.
                              When it touched my ears
he dubbed me *Paganinny* and it hurt.
I did then, and do now, choke back my tears –

Wi' 'air like that you ought to wear a skirt!

If I'd got a violin for every day
he'd said *weer's thi fiddle?* at my flowing hair
I'd have a whole string orchestra to play
romantic background as once more I'm there
where we went for my forced fortnightly clip
now under new, less shearing, ownership,
and in the end it's that that makes me cry –

JOE'S SALOON's become KURL UP & DYE!

Still

Tugging my forelock fathoming Xenophon
grimed Greek exams with grease and lost me marks,
so I whisper when the barber asks *Owt on?*
No, thank you! YES! Dad's voice behind me barks.

They made me wear dad's hair-oil to look 'smart'.
A parting scored the grease like some slash scar.
Such aspirations hair might have for ART
were lopped, and licked by dollops from his jar.

And if the page I'm writing on has smears
they're not the sort to lose me marks for mess
being self-examination's grudging tears
soaked into the blotter, Nothingness,
on seeing the first still I'd ever seen
of Rudolph Valentino, father, O
now, *now* I know why you used *Brilliantine*
to slick back your black hair so long ago.

A Good Read

That summer it was Ibsen, Marx and Gide.

I got one of his you-stuck-up-bugger looks:

ah sometimes think you read too many books.
ah nivver 'ad much time for a good read.

Good read! I bet! Your programme at United!
The labels on your whisky or your beer!
You'd never get unbearably excited
poring over Kafka or King Lear.
The only score you'd bother with 's your darts,
or fucking football . . .

                               (All this in my mind.)

I've come round to your position on 'the Arts'
but put it down in poems, that's the bind.

These poems about you, dad, should make good reads
for the bus you took from Beeston into town
for people with no time like you in Leeds –

once I'm writing I can't put you down!

Isolation

I cried once as a boy when I'd to leave her
at Christmas in the fourth year of the War,
taken to Killingbeck with scarlet fever,
but don't cry now, although I see once more
from the window of the York–Leeds diesel back
for her funeral, my place of quarantine,

and don't, though I notice by the same railtrack
hawthorns laden with red berries as they'd been
when we'd seen them the day that we returned
from the hospital on this same train together
and she taught me a country saying that she'd learned
as a child: *Berries bode bad winter weather!*

and don't, though the fresh grave's flecked with sleet,
and dad, with every fire back home switched on, 's frozen,
       and don't,
            until I hear him bleat
round the ransacked house for his long johns.

Continuous

James Cagney was the one up both our streets.
His was the only art we ever shared.
A gangster film and choc ice were the treats
that showed about as much love as he dared.

He'd be my own age now in '49!
The hand that glinted with the ring he wore,
his father's, tipped the cold bar into mine
just as the organist dropped through the floor.

He's on the platform lowered out of sight
to organ music, this time on looped tape,
into a furnace with a blinding light
where only his father's ring will keep its shape.

I wear it now to Cagneys on my own
and sense my father's hands cupped round my treat –

they feel as though they've been chilled to the bone
from holding my ice cream all through *White Heat*.

Clearing

I

The ambulance, the hearse, the auctioneers
clear all the life of that loved house away.
The hard-earned treasures of some 50 years
sized up as junk, and shifted in a day.

A stammerer died here and I believe
this front room with such ghosts taught me my trade.
Now strangers chip the paintwork as they heave
the spotless piano that was never played.
The fingerprints they leave mam won't wipe clean
nor politely ask them first to wipe their boots,
nor coax her trampled soil patch back to green
after they've trodden down the pale spring shoots.

I'd hope my mother's spirit wouldn't chase
her scattered household, even if it could.
How could she bear it when she saw no face
stare back at her from that long polished wood?

II

The landlord's glad to sell. The neighbourhood,
he fears, being mostly black, 's now on the skids.
The gate my father made from bread-tray wood
groans at the high jinks of Jamaican kids.

Bless this house's new black owners, and don't curse
that reggae booms through rooms where you made hush
for me to study in (though I wrote verse!)
and wouldn't let my sister use the flush!

The hearse called at the front, the formal side.
Strangers used it, doctors, and the post.
It had a show of flowers till you died.
You'll have to use the front if you're a ghost,
though it's as flat and bare as the back yard,
a beaten hard square patch of sour soil.

Hush!
      Haunt me, and not the house!
                            I've got to lard
my ghosts' loud bootsoles with fresh midnight oil.

Illuminations

The two machines on Blackpool's Central Pier,
The Long Drop and *The Haunted House* gave me
my thrills the holiday that post-war year
but my father watched me spend impatiently:

Another tanner's worth, but then no more!

But I sneaked back the moment that you napped.
50 weeks of ovens, and 6 years of war
made you want sleep and ozone, and you snapped:

Bugger the machines! Breathe God's fresh air!

I sulked all week, and wouldn't hold your hand.
I'd never heard you mention God, or swear,
and it took me until now to understand.

I see now all the piled old pence turned green,
enough to hang the murderer all year
and stare at millions of ghosts in the machine –

The penny dropped in time! Wish you were here!

II

We built and bombed Boche stalags on the sands,
or hunted for beached starfish on the rocks
and some days ended up all holding hands
gripping the pier machine that gave you shocks.
The current would connect. We'd feel the buzz
ravel our loosening ties to one tense grip,
the family circle, one continuous US!
That was the first year on my scholarship
and I'd be the one who'd make that circuit short.
I lectured them on neutrons and Ohm's Law
and other half-baked Physics I'd been taught.
I'm sure my father felt I was a bore!

Two dead, but current still flows through us three
though the circle takes for ever to complete –
eternity, annihilation, me,
that small bright charge of life where they both meet.

III

The family didn't always feel together.
Those silent teas with all of us apart
when no one spoke except about the weather
and not about his football or my art.

And in those silences the grating sound
of father's celery, the clock's loud tick,
the mine subsidence from deep underground,
mi mam's loose bottom teeth's relentless click.

And when, I'm told, St James's came to fetch her,
My teeth! were the final words my mother said.
Being without them, even on a stretcher,
was more undignified than being dead.

Ay! I might have said, *and put her in her box
dressed in that long gown she bought to wear,
not to be outclassed by those posh frocks,
at her son's next New York première!*

Turns

I thought it made me look more 'working class'
(as if a bit of chequered cloth could bridge that gap!)
I did a turn in it before the glass.
My mother said: *It suits you, your dad's cap.*
(She preferred me to wear suits and part my hair:
You're every bit as good as that lot are!)

All the pension queue came out to stare.
Dad was sprawled beside the postbox (still VR),
his cap turned inside up beside his head,
smudged H A H in purple Indian ink
and Brylcreem slicks displayed so folk might think
he wanted charity for dropping dead.

He never begged. For nowt! Death's reticence
crowns his life's, and *me*, I'm opening my trap
to busk the class that broke him for the pence
that splash like brackish tears into our cap.

Punchline

No! Revolution never crossed your mind!
For the kids who never made it through the schools
the Northern working class escaped the grind
as boxers or comedians, or won the pools.

Not lucky, no physique, too shy to joke,
you scraped together almost 3 weeks' pay
to buy a cast-off uke that left you broke.
You mastered only two chords, G and A!

That's why when I've heard George Formby that I've wept.
I'd always wondered what that thing was for,
I now know was a plectrum, that you'd kept,
but kept hidden, in your secret condom drawer.

The day of your cremation which I missed
I saw an old man strum a uke he'll never play,
cap spattered with tossed dimes. I made a fist
round my small change, your son, and looked away.

Currants

I

An Eccles cake's my *petite madeleine*!

On Sundays dad stoked up for next week's bake
and once took me along to be 'wi' t'men'.

One Eccles needs the currants you could take
in a hand imagined cupped round a girl's breast.
Between barrels of dried fruit and tubs of lard
I hunched and watched, and thought of girls undressed
and wondered what it meant when cocks got hard.
As my daydream dropped her silky underclothes,
from behind I smelt my father next to me.

Sweat dropped into the currants from his nose:

Go on! 'ave an 'andful. It's all free.

Not this barrel though. Your sweat's gone into it.
I'll go and get my handful from another.

I saw him poise above the currants and then spit:

Next Sunday you can stay 'ome wi' yer mother!

II

At dawn I hear him hawk up phlegm and cough
before me or my mother are awake.
He pokes the grate, makes tea, and then he's off
to stoke the ovens for my Eccles cake.

I smell my father, wallowing in bed,
dripping salt no one will taste into his dough,
and clouds of currants spiral in my head
and like drowsy autumn insects come and go
darkening the lightening skylight and the walls.

My veins grow out of me like tough old vines
and grapes, each bunch the weight of a man's balls
picked by toiling Greeks and Levantines,
are laid out somewhere open air and warm
where there might be also women, sun, blue sky

overcast as blackened currants swarm
into my father's hard 'flies' cemetery'.

Note. An Eccles cake was called a 'flies' cemetery' by children.

Breaking the Chain

The mams pig-sick of oilstains in the wash
wished for their sons a better class of gear,
'wear their own clothes into work' but not go posh,
go up a rung or two but settle near.

This meant the drawing office to the dads,
same place of work, but not blue-collar, white.
A box like a medal case went round the lads
as, one by one, their mams pushed them as 'bright'

My dad bought it, from the last dad who still owed
the dad before, for a whole week's wage and drink.
I was brought down out of bed to have bestowed
the polished box wrapped in the *Sporting Pink*.

Looking at it now still breaks my heart!
The gap his gift acknowledged then 's as wide as
eternity, but I still can't bear to part
with these never passed on, never used, dividers.

Changing at York

A directory that runs from B to V,
the Yellow Pages' entries for HOTELS
and TAXIS torn out, the smell of dossers' pee,
saliva in the mouthpiece, whisky smells –
I remember, now I have to phone,
squashing a *Daily Mail* half full of chips,
to tell the son I left at home alone
my train's delayed, and get cut off by the pips,
how, phoning his mother, late, a little pissed,
changing at York, from some place where I'd read,
I used 2p to lie about the train I'd missed
and ten more to talk my way to some girl's bed
and, in this same kiosk with the stale, sour breath
of queuing callers, drunk, cajoling, lying,
consoling his grampa for his granny's death,
how I heard him, for the first time ever, crying.

Marked With D.

When the chilled dough of his flesh went in an oven
not unlike those he fuelled all his life,
I thought of his cataracts ablaze with Heaven
and radiant with the sight of his dead wife,
light streaming from his mouth to shape her name,
'not Florence and not Flo but always Florrie'.
I thought how his cold tongue burst into flame
but only literally, which makes me sorry,
sorry for his sake there's no Heaven to reach.
I get it all from Earth my daily bread
but he hungered for release from mortal speech
that kept him down, the tongue that weighed like lead.

The baker's man that no one will see rise
and England made to feel like some dull oaf
is smoke, enough to sting one person's eyes
and ash (not unlike flour) for one small loaf.

A Piece of Cake

This New York baker's bread 's described as 'Swiss'
though it's said there's something Nazi in their past.
But the cheesecake that they make 's the best there is.
It's made fresh every day and sells out fast.

My kids are coming so I buy one too,
and ask for a WELCOME frosted on the top.
I watch the tube squeeze out the script in blue.
It has my father's smell, this German's shop,
as he concentrates on his ice craftsmanship
that cost him weeks of evenings to complete,
a cake with V signs, spitfires, landing strip,
that took too many pains to cut and eat
to welcome home a niece back from the WAAFs.

Already I feel the cake stick in my throat!

The icing tube flows freely and then coughs.

The frosting comes out Gothic and reads: 𝕿𝕺𝕯!

The Morning After

I

The fire left to itself might smoulder weeks.
Phone cables melt. Paint peels from off back gates.
Kitchen windows crack; the whole street reeks
of horsehair blazing. Still it celebrates.

Though people weep, their tears dry from the heat.
Faces flush with flame, beer, sheer relief
and such a sense of celebration in our street
for me it still means joy though banked with grief.

And that, now clouded, sense of public joy
with war-worn adults wild in their loud fling
has never come again since as a boy
I saw Leeds people dance and heard them sing.

There's still that dark, scorched circle on the road.
The morning after kids like me helped spray
hissing upholstery spring-wire that still glowed
and cobbles boiling with black gas-tar for V J.

II

The Rising Sun was blackened on those flames.
The jabbering tongues of fire consumed its rays.
Hiroshima, Nagasaki, were mere names
for us small boys who gloried in our blaze.

The blood-red ball, first burnt to blackout shreds,
took hovering batwing on the bonfire's heat
above the *Rule Britannias* and the bobbing heads
of the V J hokey-cokey in our street.

The kitchen blackout cloth became a cloak
for me to play at fiend Count Dracula in.
I swirled it near the fire. It filled with smoke.
Heinz ketchup dribbled down my vampire's chin.

That circle of scorched cobbles scarred with tar 's
a night-sky globe nerve-wrackingly all black,
both hemispheres entire but with no stars,
an Archerless zilch, a Scaleless zodiac.

Old Soldiers

Last years of Empire and the fifth of War
and CAMP coffee extract on the kitchen table.
The Sikh that served the officer I saw
on the label in the label in the label
continuously cloned beyond my eyes,
beyond the range of any human staring,
down to amoeba, atom, neutron size
but the turbaned bearer never lost his bearing
and nothing shook the bottle off his tray.
Through all infinity and down to almost zero
he holds out and can't die or fade away
loyal to the breakfasting Scots hero.

But since those two high summer days
the US dropped the World's first A-bombs on,
from that child's forever what returns my gaze
is a last chuprassy with all essence gone.

A Close One

Hawsers. Dirigibles. Searchlight. *Messerschmitts.*
Half let go. Half rake dark nowt to find . . .

Day old bereavement debris of a blitz
there's been no shelter from, no *all clear* whined.

Our cellar 'refuge room' made anti-gas.
Damp sand that smelled of graves not Morecambe Bay.
Air Raid Precautions out of *Kensitas.*
A Victory jig-saw on Fry's Cocoa tray.
Sandwiches. Snakes & Ladders. Thermos flask.

Sirens, then silences, then bombers' drone.
Long whistles. Windows gone. Each time I'd ask
which one was the Jerry, which our own.

How close we were with death's wings overhead!

How close we were not several hours ago.

These lines to hold the still too living dead –

my Redhill container, my long-handled hoe.

'Testing the Reality'

I could count to a ragged 20 but no higher.
The flocking birds she taught me numbers by
so crammed church roof and belfry, cross and spire
their final taking off blacked Beeston's sky.

There must have been 10,000 there or more.
They picketed piercingly the passing of each day
and shrilly hailed the first new light they saw
and hour after hour their numbers grew
till, on a Sunday morning, they all flew away
as suddenly as her 70 years would do.

The day that fledged her with the wings of night
made all her days flock to it, and as one
beyond all sight, all hearing, taste, smell, touch,
they soared away and, soaring, blocked the light
of what they steered their course by from her son,
the last soul still unhatched left in the clutch.

The Effort

'The atom bomb was in manufacture before the first automatic
washing machine.'

(Tillie Olsen, *Silences*)

They took our iron railings down to dump
on Dresden as one more British bomb,
but mam cajoled the men to leave a stump
to hitch the line she hung the washing from.
So three inches didn't end in German flesh.
It was the furthest from surrender when she flew
a rope full of white Y-fronts, dazzling, fresh
from being stewed all day with dolly blue
in the cellar set-pot. Her ferocious pride
would only let quite spotless clothes outside.

Washes that made her tender hands red raw
we do nowadays in no time by machine.
No one works so hard to keep things clean
so it's maybe just as well she'd got to die
before the latest in bombardments and before
our world of minimum iron and spin dry.

Bye-Byes

The judder of energy when I jump
I laugh to see immediately pass
into the titmouse wired to a mossy stump
who taps his blunt beak on the dusty glass.

She wants me to leave 'this minute' but I won't
drawn to the faded feathers in glass cases
where grown-ups see what toddlers like me don't,
imposed on stuffed creation, their own faces.

Say bye-bye, our Tony, that's enough!
We've got to buy some liver for dad's tea,
Say bye-bye . . . sanderling, bye-bye . . . ruff!
I won't say anything, and wriggle free.

Sensing her four-year-old's about to cry
she buys me a postcard with the dodo on it.
43 years on this filial sonnet
lets the tears she staunched then out: Bye-bye!

Blocks

A droning vicar bores the congregation
and misquotes *Ecclesiastes* Chapter 3.
If anyone should deliver an oration
it should be me, her son, in poetry.

All the family round me start to sob.
For all my years of Latin and of Greek
they'd never seen the point of 'for a job',
I'm not prepared to stand up now and speak.

A time to . . . plough back into the soil
the simple rhymes that started at her knee,
the poetry, that 'sedentary toil'
that began, when her lap was warm, with ABC.

Blocks with letters. Lettered block of stone.
I have to move the blocks to say farewell.

I hear the family cry, the vicar drone
and VALE, MATER 's all that I can spell.

Jumper

When I want some sort of human metronome
to beat calm celebration out of fear
like that when German bombs fell round our home
it's my mother's needles, knitting, that I hear,
the click of needles steady though walls shake.
The stitches, plain or purl, were never dropped.
Bombs fell all that night until daybreak
but, not for a moment, did the knitting stop.
Though we shivered in the cellar-shelter's cold
and the whistling bombs sent shivers through the walls
I know now why she made her scared child hold
the skeins she wound so calmly into balls.

We open presents wrapped before she died.
With that same composure shown in that attack
she'd known the time to lay her wools aside –

the jumper I open 's shop-bought, and is black!

Bringing Up

It was a library copy otherwise
you'd've flung it in the fire in disgust.
Even cremation can't have dried the eyes
that wept for weeks about my 'sordid lust'.

The undertaker would have thought me odd
or I'd've put my book in your stiff hand.
You'd've been embarrassed though to meet your God
clutching those poems of mine that you'd like banned.

I thought you could hold my *Loiners*, and both burn!

And there together in the well wrought urn,
what's left of you, the poems of your child,
devoured by one flame, unreconciled,
like soots on washing, black on bone-ash white.

Maybe you see them in a better light!

But I still see you weeping, your hurt looks:

You weren't brought up to write such mucky books!

Timer

Gold survives the fire that's hot enough
to make you ashes in a standard urn.
An envelope of coarse official buff
contains your wedding ring which wouldn't burn.

Dad told me I'd to tell them at St James's
that the ring should go in the incinerator.
That 'eternity' inscribed with both their names is
his surety that they'd be together, 'later'.

I signed for the parcelled clothing as the son,
the cardy, apron, pants, bra, dress –

the clerk phoned down: *6-8-8-3-1?*
Has she still her ring on? (Slight pause) *Yes!*

It's on my warm palm now, your burnished ring!

I feel your ashes, head, arms, breasts, womb, legs,
sift through its circle slowly, like that thing
you used to let me watch to time the eggs.

Fire-eater

My father speaking was like conjurors I'd seen
pulling bright silk hankies, scarves, a flag
up out of their innards, red, blue, green,
so many colours it would make me gag.

Dad's eldest brother had a shocking stammer.
Dad punctuated sentence ends with but . . .
Coarser stuff than silk they hauled up grammar
knotted together deep down in their gut.

Theirs are the acts I nerve myself to follow.
I'm the clown sent in to clear the ring.
Theirs are the tongues of fire I'm forced to swallow
then bring back knotted, one continuous string
igniting long-pent silences, and going back
to Adam fumbling with Creation's names;
and though my vocal cords get scorched and black
there'll be a constant singing from the flames.

Pain-Killers

I

My father haunts me in the old men that I find
holding the shop-queues up by being slow.
It's always a man like him that I'm behind
just when I thought the pain of him would go
reminding me perhaps it never goes,
with his pension book kept utterly pristine
in a plastic wrapper labelled *Pantihose*
as if they wouldn't pay if it weren't clean,

or learning to shop so late in his old age
and counting his money slowly from a purse
I'd say from its ornate clasp and shade of beige
was his dead wife's glasses' case. I curse,
but silently, secreting pain, at this delay,
the acid in my gut caused by dad's ghost –
I've got aerogrammes to buy. My love's away!
And the proofs of *Pain-Killers* to post!

II

Going for pills to ease the pain I get
from the Post Office on Thursdays, Pension Day,
the chemist's also gives me cause to fret
at more of my dad's ghosts, and more delay
as they queue for their prescriptions without hopes
and go looking for the old cures on the shelves,
stumbling into pyramids of scented soaps
they once called cissy when they felt 'themselves'.

There are more than in the Post Office in BOOTS
and I try to pass the time behind such men
by working out the Latin and Greek roots
of cures, the *san-* that's in *Sanatogen*,
compounds derived from *derm-* for teenage spots,
suntan creams and lotions prefixed *sol-*
while a double of my dad takes three wild shots
at pronouncing PARACETAMOL.

Background Material

My writing desk. Two photos, mam and dad.
A birthday, him. Their ruby wedding, her.
Neither one a couple and both bad.
I make out what's behind them from the blur.

Dad's in our favourite pub, now gone for good.
My father and his background are both gone,
but hers has my Welsh cottage and a wood
that still shows those same greens eight summers on,
though only the greenness of it 's stayed the same.

Though one of them 's in colour and one 's not,
the two are joined, apart from their shared frame,
by what, for photographers, would mar each shot:

in his, if you look close, the gleam, the light,
me in his blind right eye, but minute size –

in hers, as though just cast from where I write,
a shadow holding something to its eyes.

THREE   Self Justification

Me a poet! My daughter with maimed limb
became a more than tolerable sprinter.
And Uncle Joe. Impediment spurred him,
the worst stammerer I've known, to be a printer.

He handset type much faster than he spoke.
Those cruel consonants, *m*s, *p*s, and *b*s
on which his jaws and spirit almost broke
flicked into order with sadistic ease.

It seems right that Uncle Joe, 'b-buckshee
from the works', supplied those scribble pads
on which I stammered my first poetry
that made me seem a cissy to the lads.

Their aggro towards me, my need of them 's
what keeps my would-be mobile tongue still tied —

aggression, struggle, loss, blank printer's ems
by which all   eloquence   gets justified.

Divisions

I

All aggro in tight clothes and skinhead crops
they think that like themselves I'm on the dole.
Once in the baths that mask of 'manhood' drops.
Their decorated skins lay bare a soul.

Teenage dole-wallah piss-up, then tattoos.
Brown Ale and boys' bravado numbs their fright –
MOTHER in ivy, blood reds and true blues
against that North East skin so sunless white.

When next he sees United lose a match,
his bovvers on, his scarf tied round his wrist,
his rash NEWCASTLE RULES will start to scratch,
he'll aerosol the walls, then go get pissed . . .

So I hope the TRUE LOVE on your arm stays true,
the MOTHER on your chest stays loved, not hated.

But most I hope for jobs for all of you –

next year your tattooed team gets relegated!

II

Wartime bunkers, runways overgrown,
streets named for the town's two England caps;
cricket played with shovelblade and stone,
the daylight's rotten props near to collapse.

HEALTH (H changed to W) FOR ALL
with its *Never Have Another Haemorrhoid*
is all that decorates the tap-room wall
of this pub for pensioners and unemployed.

The Brewery that owns this place supports
only the unambiguously 'male'
Northern working class spectator sports
that suit the image of its butch *Brown Ale*,
that puts hair on your chest, and makes you fight,
and when you're legless makes a man of you!

The *Brown Ale* drinkers watch me as I write:

one front door orange in a row all blue!

History Classes

Past scenic laybys and stag warning signs
the British borderlands roll into view.

They read: *Beware of Unexploded Mines*!
I tell my children that was World War II.

They want to walk or swim. We pick up speed.
My children boo the flash of each NO ENTRY:

High seas, and shooting, uniform or tweed,
Ministry of Defence, or landed gentry.

Danger flags from valley mills that throve,
after a fashion, on the Empire's needs.

Their own clothes spun in India they wove
the Colonel's khaki and the blue blood's tweeds.

Mill angelus, and church tower twice as high.
One foundry cast the work- and rest-day bells –

the same red cotton 's in the flags that fly
for ranges, revolutions, and rough swells.

Stately Home

'Behold Land-Interest's compound Man & Horse.'
                                        (Ebenezer Elliott)

Those bad old days of 'rapine and of reif!'
Northumberland's peles still seeping with old wars —
this year's lawful lord and last year's thief,
those warring centaurs, scratch their unscabbed sores.

But here, horned koodoo and okapi skulls,
the family's assegais, a Masai shield,
the head of one of Chillingham's white bulls,
this month's *Tatler*, *Horse & Hound*, *The Field*.

Churned earth translucent Meissen, dusted Spode
displayed on Sundays for the pence it makes,
paintings of beasts they'd shot at or they'd rode,
cantered grabbed acres on, won local stakes,
once all one man's debatable demesne,
a day's hard ride from Cheviot to sea —

His scion, stretching back to Charlemagne,
stiff-backed, lets us put down 40p.

Lines to my Grandfathers

I

Ploughed parallel as print the stony earth.
The straight stone walls defy the steep grey slopes.
The place's rightness for my mother's birth
exceeds the pilgrim grandson's wildest hopes –

Wilkinson farmed Thrang Crag, Martindale.

Horner was the Haworth signalman.

Harrison kept a pub with home-brewed ale:

fell farmer, railwayman, and *publican*,

and he, while granma slaved to tend the vat
graced the rival bars 'to make comparisons',
Queen's Arms, the Duke of this, the Duke of that,
while his was known as just 'The Harrisons''.

He carried cane and *guineas*, no coin baser!
He dressed the gentleman beyond his place
and paid in gold for beer and whisky chaser
but took his knuckleduster, 'just in case'.

II

The one who lived with us was grampa Horner
who, I remember, when a sewer rat
got driven into our dark cellar corner
booted it to pulp and squashed it flat.

He cobbled all our boots. I've got his last.
We use it as a doorstop on warm days.
My present is propped open by their past
and looks out over straight and narrow ways:

the way one ploughed his land, one squashed a rat,
kept railtracks clear, or, dressed up to the nines,
with waxed moustache, gold chain, his cane, his hat,
drunk as a lord could foot it on straight lines.

Fell farmer, railwayman and publican,
I strive to keep my lines direct and straight,
and try to make connections where I can –

the knuckleduster's now my paperweight!

The Earthen Lot

for Alistair Elliot

'From Ispahan to Northumberland, there is no building that
does not show the influence of that oppressed and neglected
herd of men.'

(William Morris, The Art of the People)

Sand, caravans, and teetering sea-edge graves.

The seaward side's for those of lowly status.
Not only gales gnaw at their names, the waves
jostle the skulls and bones from their quietus.

The Church is a solid bulwark for their betters
against the scouring sea-salt that erodes
these chiselled sandstone formal Roman letters
to flowing calligraphic Persian odes,
singing of sherbert, sex in Samarkand,
with Hafiz at the hammams and harems,
O anywhere but bleak Northumberland
with responsibilities for others' dreams!

Not for the Northern bard the tamarinds
where wine is always cool, and *kusi* hot –

his line from Omar scrivened by this wind 's:

Some could articulate, while others not.

(Newbiggin-by-the-Sea 1977)

Remains

for Robert Woof and Fleur Adcock

Though thousands traipse round Wordsworth's Lakeland
  shrine
imbibing bardic background, they don't see
nailed behind a shutter one lost line
with intimations of mortality
and immortality, but so discrete
it's never trespassed on 'the poet's' aura,
nor been scanned, as it is, five strong verse feet.

W. Martin's work needs its restorer,
and so from 1891 I use
the paperhanger's one known extant line
as the culture that I need to start off mine
and honour his one visit by the Muse,
then hide our combined labours underground
so once again it might be truly said
in words from Grasmere written by the dead:

our heads will be happen cold when this is found.

W. Martin
paperhanger
4 July 1891

Dichtung und Wahrheit

for Marcelino Dos Santos (Frelimo)
Dar-es-Salaam 1971

Frelimo's fluent propagandist speaks
the cloven tongues of four colonial powers:
French and Spanish, Portuguese and ours,
plus Makonde *one* of Mozambique's,
and swears in each the war will soon be won.
He speaks of 'pen & sword', quotes Mao's phrase
about 'all power' the moment his guests gaze
on the 14–18 bronze with Maxim gun.

Dulciloquist Dos Santos, swear to them
whose languages you'll never learn to speak
that tongues of fire at a 1000 rpm
is not the final eloquence you seek.

Spondaic or dactylic those machines
and their dry scansions mean that truths get lost,

and a *pravda* empty as its magazines
is Kalashnikov PK 's flash Pentecost.

Art & Extinction

'When I hear of the destruction of a species I feel as if all the works of some great writer had perished.'

(Theodore Roosevelt, 1899)

1. *The Birds of America*

(i) John James Audubon (1785–1851)

The struggle to preserve once spoken words
from already too well-stuffed taxonomies
is a bit like Audubon's when painting birds,
whose method an admirer said was this:
Kill 'em, wire 'em, paint 'em, kill a fresh 'un!

The plumage even of the brightest faded.
The artist had to shoot in quick succession
till all the feathers were correctly shaded.

Birds don't pose for pictures when alive!
Audubon's idea of restraint,
doing the Pelican, was 25
dead specimens a day for *one* in paint.

By using them do we save words or not?

As much as Audubon's art could save a,
say, godwit, or a grackle, which he shot
and then saw 'multiplied by Havell's graver'.

(ii) Weeki Wachee

Duds doomed to join the dodo: the dugong,
talonless eagles, croc, gimp manatee,
here, courtesy Creation's generous strong,
the losers of thinned jungle and slicked sea.

Many's the proud chieftain used to strut
round shady clearings of dark festooned teak
with twenty cockatoo tails on his nut,
macaw plumes à la mode, rainforest chic.

Such gladrag gaudies safe in quarantine
and spared at least their former jungle fate
of being blowpiped for vain primitives to preen
now race a tightrope on one roller skate.

A tanned sophomore, these ghettoed birds' Svengali,
shows glad teeth, evolved for smiling, as macaws
perform their deft Darwinian finale
by hoisting the Stars and Stripes for our applause.

(iii) Standards

in hopeful anticipation of the bicentenary of the national
emblem of the United States of America, *Haliaaetus Falco
Leucocephalus*, 1782–1982

'The bald eagle is likewise a large, strong, and very active bird,
but an execrable tyrant: he supports his assumed dignity and
grandeur by rapine and violence, extorting unreasonable tribute
and subsidy from the feathered nations.'

(William Bartram, Travels, 1791)

'Our standard with the eagle stands for us.
It waves in the breeze in almost every clime.'

(The flag, not *Falco Leucocephalus*
poised in its dying on the brink of time!)

Rejecting Franklin's turkey for a bird that *flies*
Congress chose the soaring eagle, called,
for its conspicuous white head, 'the bald'.

Now the turkey's thriving and the eagle dies!

When the last stinks in its eyrie, or falls slow,
when the very last bald eagle goes the way
of all the unique fauna, it won't know
the Earth it plummets to 's the USA.

But will still wing over nations as the ghost
on money, and the mountainous US Post.

much as sunlight shining through the British pound
showed PEACE with her laurels, white on a green ground.

2. *Loving Memory*

for Teresa Stratas

The fosses where Caractacus fought Rome
blend with grey bracken and become a blur
above the Swedish Nightingale's last home.

Somehow my need for you makes me seek her.

The Malverns darken as the dusk soaks in.
The rowan berries' dark red glaze grows dull.
The harvest moon's scraped silver and bruised tin
is only one night off from being full.

Death keeps all hours, but graveyards close at nights.
I hurry past the Malvern Hospital
where a nurse goes round small wards and puts on lights
and someone there's last night begins to fall.

'The oldest rocks this earth can boast', these hills,
packed with extinction, make me burn for you.

I ask two women leaving with dead daffodils:
Where's Jenny Lind's grave, please? They both say: *Who?*

3. *Looking Up*

for Philip, Terry, and Will Sharpe and the bicentenary of the
birth of Peter Mark Roget (1779–1869)

All day till it grows dark I sit and stare
over Herefordshire hills and into Wales.
Reflections of red coals thrown on the air
blossom to brightness as the daylight fails.

An uncharred cherry flaunts a May of flames.
Like chaffinches and robins tongues of fire
flit with the burden of Creation's names
but find no new apostles to inspire.

Bar a farmhouse TV aerial or two,
the odd red bus, the red Post Office van,
this must have been exactly Roget's view,
good Dr Roget, the *Thesaurus* man.

Roget died here, but 90 when he died
of natural causes, twice as old as me.

Of his six synonyms for suicide
I set myself alight with safe suttee.

4. *Killing Time*

Among death-protected creatures in a case,
'The Earth's Endangered Species' on display
at a jam-packed terminal at JFK,
killing time again, I see my face
with Hawksbill Turtle, scrimshawed spermwhale bone,
the Margay of the family *Felidae*,
that, being threatened, cost the earth to buy.

And now with scientists about to clone
the long-haired mammoth back from Soviet frost,
my reflection's on the species the World's lost,
or will be losing in a little while,
which, as they near extinction, grow in worth,
the leopard, here a bag and matching purse,
the dancing shoes that were Nile crocodile,

the last *Felis Pardalis* left on Earth,

the poet preserved beneath deep permaverse.

5. *Dark Times*

That the *Peppered Moth* was white and now is dark 's
a lesson in survival for Mankind.

Around the time Charles Darwin had declined
the dedication of *Das Kapital* by Marx
its predators could spot it on the soot,
but Industrial Revolution and Evolution taught
the moth to black its wings and not get caught
where all of Nature perished, or all but.

When lichens lighten some old smoke-grimed trees
and such as Yorkshire's millstacks now don't burn
and fish nose waters stagnant centuries,
can *Biston Carbonaria* relearn,

if Man's awakened consciousness succeeds
in turning all these tides of blackness back
and diminishing the need for looking black,

to flutter white again above new Leeds?

6. *t'Ark*

Silence and poetry have their own reserves.
The numbered creatures flourish less and less.
A language near extinction best preserves
the deepest grammar of our nothingness.

Not only dodo, oryx and great auk
waddled on their tod to t'monster ark,
but 'leg', 'night', 'origin' in crushed people's talk,
tongues of fire last witnessed mouthing: *dark*!

Now when the future couldn't be much darker,
there being fewer epithets for sun,
and Cornish and the Togoland *Restsprache*
name both the animals and hunter's gun,
celebrate before things go too far
Papua's last reported manucode,
the pygmy hippo of the Côte d'Ivoire,
and Upper Guinea's oviparous toad –

(or mourn in Latin their imminent death,
then translate these poems into *cynghanedd*.)

¶

Facing North

'The North begins inside.'
(Louis MacNeice)

God knows why of all rooms I'd to choose
the dark one facing North for me to write,
liking as I do air, light and views,
though there's air in the North Wind that rocks the light
I have to keep on, all year round, all day;
nor why, despite a climate I profess to hate,
and years spent overseas, I stay,
and, when I start to pack, procrastinate.

The North Wind's part of it and when it blows
my shutters rattle and the front door slams
like memory shutting out half what it knows.
Here I poured huge passion into aerogrammes,
the lightest paper loaded with new hope
that made the old pain seem, on looking back,
seen through the wrong end of the telescope
making it so small I soon lost track.

The window's open to the winter's chill,
to air, to breezes and strong gusts that blow
my paper lantern nothing will keep still
and let me make things happen in its O.
When the circle, where my hand moves over white
with red and green advances on black ink,
first swung like this it gave me such a fright
I felt I was on a ship about to sink.

Now years of struggle make me concentrate
when it throws up images of planets hurled,
still glowing, off their courses, and a state
where there's no gravity to hold the world.
I have to hold on when I think such things
and weather out these feelings so that when
the wind drops and the light no longer swings
I can focus on an Earth that still has men,

in this flooded orchestra where elbow grease,
deep thought, long practice and much sweat
gave me some inkling of an inner peace
I'd never found with women till I met
the one I wrote all those air letters for
and she's the one I'm needing as I see
the North Wind once more strip my sycamore
and whip the last leaves off my elder tree.

Now when the wind flays my wild garden of its green
and blows, whistling through the flues, its old reminder
of the two cold poles all places are between,
though where she lives the climate's a lot kinder,
and starts the lightbulb swinging to and fro,
and keeps it swinging, switched off, back and forth,
I feel the writing room I'm leaving grow
dark, and then darker with the whole view North.

A Kumquat for John Keats

Today I found the right fruit for my prime,
not orange, not tangelo, and not lime,
nor moon-like globes of grapefruit that now hang
outside our bedroom, nor tart lemon's tang
(though last year full of bile and self-defeat
I wanted to believe no life was sweet)
nor the tangible sunshine of the tangerine,
and no incongruous citrus ever seen
at greengrocers' in Newcastle or Leeds
mis-spelt by the spuds and mud-caked swedes,
a fruit an older poet might substitute
for the grape John Keats thought fit to be Joy's fruit,
when, two years before he died, he tried to write
how Melancholy dwelled inside Delight,
and if he'd known the citrus that I mean
that's not orange, lemon, lime or tangerine,
I'm pretty sure that Keats, though he had heard
'of candied apple, quince and plum and gourd'
instead of 'grape against the palate fine'
would have, if he'd known it, plumped for mine,
this Eastern citrus scarcely cherry size
he'd bite just once and then apostrophize
and pen one stanza how the fruit had all
the qualities of fruit before the Fall,
but in the next few lines be forced to write
how Eve's apple tasted at the second bite,
and if John Keats had only lived to be,
because of extra years, in need like me,
at 42 he'd help me celebrate
that Micanopy kumquat that I ate
whole, straight off the tree, sweet pulp and sour skin
or was it sweet outside, and sour within?
For however many kumquats that I eat

I'm not sure if it's flesh or rind that's sweet,
and being a man of doubt at life's mid-way
I'd offer Keats some kumquats and I'd say:
You'll find that one part's sweet and one part's tart:
say where the sweetness or the sourness start.
I find I can't, as if one couldn't say
exactly where the night became the day,
which makes for me the kumquat taken whole
best fruit, and metaphor, to fit the soul
of one in Florida at 42 with Keats
crunching kumquats, thinking, as he eats
the flesh, the juice, the pith, the pips, the peel,
that this is how a full life ought to feel,
its perishable relish prick the tongue,
when the man who savours life 's no longer young,
the fruits that were his futures far behind.
Then it's the kumquat fruit expresses best
how days have darkness round them like a rind,
life has a skin of death that keeps its zest.

History, a life, the heart, the brain
flow to the taste buds and flow back again.
That decade or more past Keats's span
makes me an older not a wiser man,
who knows that it's too late for dying young,
but since youth leaves some sweetnesses unsung,
he's granted days and kumquats to express
Man's Being ripened by his Nothingness.
And it isn't just the gap of sixteen years,
a bigger crop of terrors, hopes and fears,
but a century of history on this earth
between John Keats's death and my own birth –
years like an open crater, gory, grim,
with bloody bubbles leering at the rim;
a thing no bigger than an urn explodes
and ravishes all silence, and all odes,
Flora asphyxiated by foul air
unknown to either Keats or Lemprière,

dehydrated Naiads, Dryad amputees
dragging themselves through slagscapes with no trees,
a shirt of Nessus fire that gnaws and eats
children half the age of dying Keats . . .

Now were you twenty five or six years old
when that fevered brow at last grew cold?
I've got no books to hand to check the dates.
My grudging but glad spirit celebrates
that all I've got to hand 's the kumquats, John,
the fruit I'd love to have your verdict on,
but dead men don't eat kumquats, or drink wine,
they shiver in the arms of Proserpine,
not warm in bed beside their Fanny Brawne,
nor watch her pick ripe grapefruit in the dawn
as I did, waking, when I saw her twist,
with one deft movement of a sunburnt wrist,
the moon, that feebly lit our last night's walk
past alligator swampland, off its stalk.
I thought of moon-juice juleps when I saw,
as if I'd never seen the moon before,
the planet glow among the fruit, and its pale light
make each citrus on the tree its satellite.

Each evening when I reach to draw the blind
stars seem the light zest squeezed through night's blac
    rind;
the night's peeled fruit the sun, juiced of its rays,
first stains, then streaks, then floods the world with days
days, when the very sunlight made me weep,
days, spent like the nights in deep, drugged sleep,
days in Newcastle by my daughter's bed,
wondering if she, or I, weren't better dead,
days in Leeds, grey days, my first dark suit,
my mother's wreaths stacked next to Christmas fruit,
and days, like this in Micanopy. Days!

As strong sun burns away the dawn's grey haze
I pick a kumquat and the branches spray

cold dew in my face to start the day.
The dawn's molasses make the citrus gleam
still in the orchards of the groves of dream.
The limes, like Galway after weeks of rain,
glow with a greenness that is close to pain,
the dew-cooled surfaces of fruit that spent
all last night flaming in the firmament.
The new day dawns. O days! My spirit greets
the kumquat with the spirit of John Keats.
O kumquat, comfort for not dying young,
both sweet and bitter, bless the poet's tongue!
I burst the whole fruit chilled by morning dew
against my palate. Fine, for 42!

I search for buzzards as the air grows clear
and see them ride fresh thermals overhead.
Their bleak cries were the first sound I could hear
when I stepped at the start of sunrise out of doors,
and a noise like last night's bedsprings on our bed
from Mr Fowler sharpening farmers' saws.

Skywriting

for David Hockney

The Californians read the sky aloud.
The Pasadena HAPPY turns to cloud!

My desk top's like a Californian pool.
Practice mirrors from the ballet school,
meditation group, karate class
dodge or lay doggo in my desk-top glass,
but the opposite gymnasia both let through
enough clear sky to flood the desk with blue
which, like purposeful deletions, smoketrails cross.

Such smoketrails would have been of sphagnum moss
if these aeroplanes were floats displayed
at Pasadena's New Year Rose Parade,
and in the air, plus HAPPY, there'd appear
as HAPPY starts dissolving, the NEW YEAR.
The seven puffs of white that made the Y
are disconnected cottonballs and sky.

As many floats as minutes are in hours
and nothing's used to make them but fresh flowers;
raw cotton (wool not being flora) sheep
go bleating round a hyacinth Bo-Peep.
A woodwardia howdah delicately sways
with jonquil rajahs turbaned with bouquets,
the Cross in crocus and in baby's breath
but no carnation Christ clamped to his death,
no battered nailheads of black onion seeds,
no spearthrust of poinsettia that bleeds.
A larkspur 'Swoonatra' in lunaria marquee
croons blue dendrobiums as do-re-mi,
a eucalyptus Calliope plays
furze and broom ta-ra-ra-boom-de-ays.

Next day in Pasadena the parade

succumbs to seconds and to Centigrade.
Mange-stricken mane and stripes moult in the heat,
the tiger's marigolds, the lion's wheat.
Poinsettia and poppy start to wilt
and deMcPhersonize the floral kilt.
Stoned teenagers in New Year t-shirts steal
the gladioli from the glockenspiel.
What struts in a sticky palm an hour or so 's
no longer the snake's pupil but a rose.

Real gardens make imaginary toads
as purple biro marks make funeral odes,
roses one huge daffodil, the clover moons,
and ferns make bars with cedar bark spitoons.
Life made out of minutes rings as true
as floragraphs of Cherokee and Sioux,
and like igloos quilted out of eglantine
1980's made from '79!

The new depth of my desk top's like a pit's!

The first stars spike its black with silver spritz.
The twilight shandygaff's a little swish
of seltzer in a lake of liquorice.
Under plexiglass the crushed polestar
's a boot-buffed Coke top stuck in Broadway tar.
Half conquered, half unconquerable space
in total darkness now reflects my face.
The space where Apollo slid into Soyuz
cries out for some strong, some tireless muse.
Like Arabella spider, I too try,
trailing these blown lines across the sky,
the creator with small letter c,
to learn to spin new webs in zero G.

And these figures lowered through my eyes
out of and into ever darkening skies,
they're not the engrossed classes opposite
floating in free fall above my pit,
feeling each other's faces like the blind,

or trying to rein still a racing mind,
nor those who've spent the new decade's first weeks
mastering self-help anti-rape techniques –
Mummers from Allendale, that's who they are!
Glum guisers with halved hogsheads of lit tar,
in costumes culled from soccer and crusade
cast crackling casks to start the new decade.
The firebarrels make a New Year blaze
that sparks a chain of beacons that are days.
The tossèd in barrels send a noisy hiss
up from the surface of my desk's abyss.
It's up to someone else, not me to write
HAPPY in this smoke across the night.

Exeunt the other mummers. 'In comes I'
sounding with short plumb my blackened sky,
blackface Narcissus whose spirit has to pass
over the desk with dark depths in its glass.

In the glass desk now no lightening spark
pricks through the shiny carbon of its dark. .
Night's caulked over the light's last penpoint chink.
The tarred creator stares at seas of ink,
and at the solstice of his silence cries aloud:

The Pasadena HAPPY turns to cloud!

And goes on repeating and repeating the same cry
until the seas of ink have all run dry.

The Call of Nature

Taos, New Mexico, 1980

for the 50th anniversary of the death of D. H. Lawrence
(1885–1930)

Juniper, aspen, blue spruce, just thawing snow
on the Sangre de Cristo mountains of New Mexico.

The trick's to get that splendid view with all
those open spaces, without the hot-dog stall,
and those who shoot their photos as they pass
might well end up with billboards saying GAS!

The pueblo people live without TV
but will let you snap their houses, for a fee.
Their men get work as extras and are bussed
to ancestral battlefields to bite the dust.
And bussed, but to snap adobes, rubber necks
get excursion visits to 'the priest of sex'.
They stay put in the bus. They smell the pine
not spritzed from aerosols but genuine,
dense in the thin air of that altitude.
They've heard about his work, and that it's rude.
Back on the valley freeway at the first motel
they forget both noble Navajo and D.H.L.
Their call of nature ends through separate doors
branded in ranch pokerwork: BRAVES! SQUAWS!

Giving Thanks

Late last night on 77th I waited
to watch the Macy mammoths get inflated
and listen to the blear-eyed children cheer
as Kermit's leg or Snoopy's limp left ear
came out of their collapse, as gas was blown
through each sagged limb, now magically regrown.

Each mammoth stirs beneath its weighted net
straining for the sky it can't have yet,
impatient to be loosed out of the dark
over the browning trees of Central Park.

From yesterday I still can feel you blow
your love all through me like some helium
that restores my true proportions, head to toe,
and lifts my body skywards. When I come
I'm out of the sandbagged nets and soar away
into release and *my* Thanksgiving Day.

Thanksgiving Day, 22 November 1979

Oh, Moon of Mahagonny!

for John Dexter

Oh, moon of Mahagonny
we now must say goodbye!

I never thought I'd live to see the day,
or smile my un-*Smile Center* sort of smile
that the Rockefellers threw a big soirée
for the cast of *Mahagonny* by Brecht/Weill.

Oh, moon of Mahagonny
we now must say goodbye!

Between mouthfuls on the ACT II EATING set
where Jacob Schmidt ate two whole calves, then burst,
the argument's: *Iranian* v. *Soviet* –
that is which caviar to boycott first!

Oh, moon of Mahagonny
we now must say goodbye!

These are the tight-belt ways they're fighting back:
each patriotic family should drive,
say, only one per person Cadillac
at the less gas-guzzling speed of 55.

All loyal alcoholics should desire
their vodka stingers without *Stolichnaya*.

Oh, moon of Mahagonny
we now must say goodbye!

To say the New York rich can't enter Heaven
(that old precinct of the poor) 's as much to say
we don't believe the PanAm 747
takes off time after time at JFK.

Oh, moon of Mahagonny
we now must say goodbye!

Oh, Marc Chagall should come back as a ghost
once he's checked who's got God's gilt entrée
and redecorate the Opera for our host
with fitter friezes for the MET foyer:

blue bread and circuses, lame Pegasi
and camels that hoopla through the needle's eye!

Oh, moon of Mahagonny
we now must say goodbye!

The Red Lights of Plenty

for the centenary of the death of Karl Marx, died London,
14 March 1883

> '. . . et asperi
> Martis sanguineas quae cohibet manus,
> quae dat belligeris foedera gentibus
> et cornu retinet divite copiam.'
> (Seneca, *Medea* 62–65)

Though aging and abused still half benign
this petrified PLENTY spilling from her horn
the Old World's edibles, the redskins' corn,
next to the Law Court's Fallout Shelter sign
the blacks and oranges of Hallowe'en.
All that motherly bounty turned to stone!
She chokes back tears of dribbling gasoline
for the future fates of countries like my own.

I stroll round Washington. November strews
red welcomes on the pavements from the trees
on Constitution and Independence Avenues
as if the least pedestrians were VIPs
or returning warlords lured inside to hack,
their lifeblood gushing out this hue of Fall
bulldozed by Buick and by Cadillac
to side drains too choked up to take it all.

Through two museums, *Science* and *Indian Arts*
something from deep below the car-choked street,
like thousands of Poe's buried tell-tale hearts
pounds with a bass and undissembled beat.
With NASA decals, necklaces by Navajo,
Japanese in groups come out to stare
at the demolition that they'd felt below
their feet, choking this chill Sunday air.

The American Wrecking Co.'s
repeatedly rammed iron wrecking ball
swinging in arcs of rhythmic tos and fros
against a scarcely-50-year-old, well-built wall
cracks cement from criss-cross steel supports,
and, floor by floor, once guaranteed to last
till time needs more museums, Justice Courts,
and enterprises space, collapses to the past.

A red light flashes many times a minute
on the Population Clock here in D.C.
to show the billions the World has in it
including those police, that black youth, me,
and, three years ago today, reached 4.5!
Each line of verse how many people born?
How many of these children will survive
crushed through the narrow end of PLENTY's horn?

And one red light for punished and for pitied
the FBI displays next to the time
flashes on whenever there's committed
somewhere in the States a serious crime,
as I imagine that it flashed on when the youth
I see handcuffed and then screeched away
to monuments of Justice, Order, Truth,
committed his, but what it was I couldn't say.

An All Souls' pumpkin rots on someone's porch.
It could be PLENTY's head, about to die,
her cornucopia a guttering torch
still hot enough to scorch the whole Earth dry.
This pumpkin lantern's gouged eyes glued
against some unbelievably bright glare
can't see, as I do, that young black pursued
then caught, the red lights hacking darkening air.

Leaves, some like menses, some volcanic hues,
whirl on successive wafts of hot CO
as Constitution and Independence Avenues

boom to the ball and chain's destructive blow
and, against Virginia, on Capital and Law
each sunset-reddened window one degree
of vast thermometers that, floor by floor,
chart our fever up to World War Three.

In a poem this long how many new souls born?
How many pendulum swings of wreckers' ball
that throbs beneath the White House on whose lawn
a giant vacuum's Hoovering the Fall?

The Heartless Art

in memoriam S.T., died 4 April 1985

Death is in your house, but I'm out here
sackclothing kumquats against the forecast freeze,
filling the hole you took two days to clear
of briars, beercans, and bleached, barkless trees,
with hackberry leaves, pine needles, stuff like that.
Next spring, when you're no longer here
we'll have the land grassed over and quite flat.

When the Southern sun starts setting it sets fast.
I've time to tip one more load if I run.
Because I know this light could be your last
I drain the day of every drop of sun.
The barrow wheel spins round with a clock's tick.
I hear, three fields away, a hunter's gun,
you, in the silence after, being sick.

I watched you, very weak, negotiate
the childproof pill jar, panting to draw breath,
and when you managed it you poured your hate
more on the poured-out contents than on death,
and, like Baptists uttering Beelzebub
syllable by syllable, spat *Meth-
a-done*, and there's also the poetic rub!

I've often heard my fellow poets (or those
who write in metres something like my own
with rhyme and rhythm, not in chopped-up prose
and brood on man's mortality) bemoan
the insufficiency of rhymes for death –
hence my syllabifying *Methadone*
instead of just saying that you fought for breath.

Maybe the main but not the only cause;
a piece of engineering I'll explain.

Each syllable *was* followed by a pause
for breathlessness, and scorn of drugs for pain.
Another reason, though, was to delay
the use of one more rhyme stored in my brain
that, alas, I'll have a use for any day.

I'd stored away this rhyme when we first met.
Knowing you crawled on hands and knees to prime
our water pump, I'll expiate one debt
by finally revealing that stored rhyme
that has the same relentlessness as death
and comes to every one of us in time
and comes to you this April full moon, SETH!

In return for all those oily working parts
you took the time and trouble to explain,
the pump that coughs, the saw that never starts,
I'll show you to distract you from the pain
you feel, except when napping, all the time
because you won't take drugs that dull the brain,
a bit about my metre, line and rhyme.

In Arthur Symons' *St Teresa* Nazaréth
is stressed on the last against its spoken flow
to engineer the contrast Jesus/Death.
Do I endorse that contrast? I don't, no!
To have a life on Earth and then want Heaven
seems like that all-night bar sign down below
that says that *Happy Hour*'s from 4 to 7.

Package lounges are like ambulances:
the Bourbon-bibber stares at us and glowers
at what he thinks are pained or pitying glances.
We don't see his face but he sees ours.
The non-dying don't see you but you see them
passing by to other rooms with flowers
as you fill the shining kidney with red phlegm.

I've left some spaces (   )[1]
benumbed by morphia and *Methadone*
until the (   )[2] of April, (   )[3]
When I began these lines could I have known
that the nurse's registration of the time
you let your spirit go with one last groan
would help complete the first and third line rhyme?

Those bits I added later. Them apart
I wrote this *in memoriam* for Seth,
meant to show him something of my art,
almost a whole week before his death.
The last thing the dying want to read,
I thought, 's a poem, and didn't show it,
and you, not dying yet, why should you need
to know the final failure of the poet?

1. how you stayed alive
2. 4th
3. 10.05

The Lords of Life

The snake our cracker neighbour had to scotch
was black and white and beautiful to watch.
I'd watched it shift its length, stay still, sashay,
shunting its flesh on shuffled vertebrae
for days before, and thought of it as 'mine'
so long had I wondered at its pliant spine.
My neighbour thinks it queer my sense of loss.
He took a branch festooned with Spanish moss,
at the cooler end of one long afternoon,
and pestled my oaksnake's head into a spoon
he flourished laughing at his dogs, then slung
the slack ladle of its life to where it hung
snagged on a branch for buzzards till, stripped bare,
it trailed like a Chinese kite-string in the air.
Waal! he exclaimed, *if ahda knowed you guys*
liked *snakes on your land* ... he turns and sighs
at such greenhornery. I'd half a mind
to say I'd checked the snake's a harmless kind
in *two* encyclopaedias but knew the looks
I'd get from him for 'talking books'. —
There's something fairy (I can hear him say)
about a guy that watches *snakes all goddam day!*
The wife he bullies says: *O Bill, let be!*
There's doers and there's watchers, maybe he ...
Ain't no doer, says he, *that's plain to see!*
I seed him sit out on their porch and read
some goddam great Encyclopaed-
ia, yeah, read! What does the fairy DO?
O Bill! she says, *not everyone's like you.*
And you'd be the first man to stand up and say
that people living in the USA
have every right to live the way they please. —
Yeah! But those guys look too young for retirees!

Nothing that I did made any sense
but I think he offered me as recompense
for battering my snake the chance to see
the alligators on his property.

Each Sunday his riding mower wouldn't stop
till every blade of grass had had its crop,
so that the bald, burned earth showed through the green
but any snake that trespassed was soon seen.
That was the front, but out there in the back
he hadn't even hacked a proper track
down to the swampy lake, his own retreat
kept as wild as the front part was kept neat.
This was his wilderness, his very own
left just as it was, rank, overgrown,
and into this he went with guns and beer
to wallow in his dreams of the frontier
and shot the gators we were seeing glide
with egrets on their backs from side to side.
The egrets ride in threes their gator skiffs,
Pharaohs' sarcophagi with hieroglyphs!
He offered me his rifle: *Wanna try?*
Go for the big ones not the smaller fry!
They've taken gators off the Endangered List.
I took aim and, deliberately, missed.
He blasted three egrets like a fairground shy
and then the gator they were ferried by.
Then we sat down at his fire and watched the day,
now reddened at the edges, drain away.
This hissing of damp logs and ringpull *Bud*
drunk from the can, his seal of brotherhood
(the sort where I'd play Abel and him Cain!)
I can't stand his beer but don't complain
as he flings them across the fire for me to catch:
round 1: the shooting, 2: the boozing match!
Each dead can he crushed flat and tossed aside.
(When I was safe back home I also tried
and found, to my great chagrin, aluminum

crushable with pressure from one thumb!)
We stare into his cookout and exchange
neighbourly nothings, gators still in range.
Liberal with his beer-cans he provokes
his gator-watching guest with racist jokes.
Did you know, sir, that gators only eat
dogs and niggers, darker sortsa meat?
But you can eat him if he won't eat you.
I'll give you a gator steak to barbecue.
(He knew that cooking's something that I *do!*)
He'd watched me cooking, and, done out of doors,
cooking could be classed among male chores.
His suspicions of me as some city loafer
who couldn't gut a mullet or stew gopher
I tried, when I felt him watching, to dispel
by letting him see me working, working well.
I make sure, when he stares over, my swing's true
when I heave the axe like I've seen rednecks do,
both hands well-balanced on the slippery haft,
or make certain that he sees me when I waft
the coals to a fierce glow with my straw hat,
the grill bars spitting goat or gator fat.
If them fireants ain't stopped with gasoline
you can say goodbye to every inch of green.
They say on the TV they'll eat their way,
if we don't check 'em, through the USA!
The 'red peril' 's what we call them bugs down here.
(A hiss for those villains from his seventh beer!)
From this house, you know, we're near enough to see
space launchings live. The wife watched on TV,
then dashed outside, and saw, with her own eyes,
'like a silver pen', she said, 'The Enterprise',
then rushed back for the message from the Prez
who'd just been wounded by some nut. He says:
We feel like giants again! *Taking over space*
has made Goliaths of the human race.
Me, I was in the rowboat, trying to relax.
I'd gotten me some chicken, 2 or 3 6-packs

like relaxing, *and I zoomed out of a snooze*
with a sudden start, the way you do with booze,
and saw our spaceship, clear as I see you,
like a bullet disappearing in the blue.
I must say that it made me mighty proud.
I sang God Bless America *out loud*
to those goddam alligators then I got
the biggest of the brutes with one sharp shot.
(But a man might get, say, lovesick, then he shoots
not one of your unendangered gator brutes
that glide so gracefully through silver ooze
and gladden gourmets in those Cross Creek stews,
and instead of potting dumb beasts like your gators
shoots the most acknowledged of all legislators,
on whose scaled back as corpse and cortège glide
the egret of the soul bums its last ride!)

Stuck goat fat's spitting from my still hot grill.
I've eaten very well, and drunk my fill,
and sip my *Early Times*, and to and fro
rock in the rocker watching ashes blow
off the white-haired charcoals and away
into the darkness of the USA.
Higher than the fireflies, not as high as stars,
the sparks fly up between the red hot bars.
I want no truck myself with outer space
except to gaze on from some earthly place
very much like this one in the South,
the taste of *Early Times* warm in my mouth.
Popping meals in pills in zero G
's not the dining that would do for me.
I'm feeling too composed to break the spell
when mosquitoes probe the veins of mine that swell
like blue earthworms. A head with sting
burrows in the blue, starts syphoning.
Let be! the watcher in me says, *Let be!*
but suddenly the doer side of me
(though my cracker neighbour couldn't, though he'd tried,

fathom if I'd got a doer side!)
swats the bastard and its legs like hair
sprout from my drop of blood on the cane chair.
The day's heat rolls away to make night thunder.
I look at the clouded planets and I wonder
if the God who blessed America's keen eye,
when He looked on that launching, chanced to spy,
in this shrinking world with far too many men,
either the cock-pecked wife who saw a pen . . .

(If I'd seen it going I'd've said
it was my snake sprayed silver, whose black head
my neighbour battered concave like a spoon,
pointing its harmless nose towards the moon,
lacquered in rigor mortis and not bent
into eternity's encirclement,
curled in a circle, sucking its own tail,
the formed continuum of female/male,
time that devours and endlessly renews,
time the open maw and what it chews,
the way it had mine chewed down here on earth,
the emblem of continuous rebirth
a bleached spine like one strand of Spanish moss –
for all the above *vide sub* Ouroboros!
All this is booktalk, buddy, mere En-
cyclopaedia know-how, not for men!) . . .

either the cock-pecked wife who saw a pen,
or the lurching rowboat where a red-faced man's
sprawled beside his shotgun and crushed cans,
who saw a bullet streak off on its trek,
and to that watching God was a mere speck,
the human mite, his rowboat lapped with blood,
the giant gator hunter killing BUD!

The Fire-Gap

A Poem with Two Tails

The fire-patrol plane's tail-fins flash.
I see it suddenly swoop low,
or maybe it's scouting out the hash
some 'crackers' round here grow.
There's nothing on our land to hide,
no marijuana here,
I think the patrol's quite satisfied
the fire-gap's bulldozed clear.
I'm not concerned what's in the air
but what's beneath my feet.
This fire-gap I walk on 's where
the snake and I will meet.
Where we live is much the same
as other land in the US,
half kept cultivated, tame,
and half left wilderness,
and living on this fire-gap
between wilderness and tilled
is the snake my neighbours want to trap;
they want 'the motherfucker' killed.
One man I know round here who's mean
would blast the hole with dynamite
or flood the lair with gasoline
and maybe set the woods alight.
Against all truculent advice
I've let the rattler stay,
and go each day with my flask of ice
to my writing shed this way.
I think the land's quite big enough
to contain both him and me
as long as the odd, discarded slough
is all of the snake I see.
But I'm aware that one day on this track

there'll be, when I'm least alert,
all six feet of diamondback
poised to do me mortal hurt,
or I might find its shrugged-off shed –
'clothes on the beach', 'gone missing',
and just when I supposed him dead
he's right behind me, hissing.
Although I know I risk my neck
each time I pass I stare
into the gopher hole to check
for signs the rattler's there.
I see the gopher's pile of dirt
with like rope-marks dragged through
and I'm at once on the alert
for the killer of the two.
Is it perverse of me to start
each morning as I pass the hole
with a sudden pounding of my heart,
my fear out of control,
my Adam's apple in a vice
so scared that I mistake
the rattle of my thermos ice
for the angry rattlesnake ?
I've started when a pine twig broke
or found I'd only been afraid
of some broken branch of dead live-oak
zig-zagged with sun and shade.
But if some barley starts to sway
against the movement of the breeze
and most blades lean the other way
that's when you'd better freeze.
If you've dragged a garden hose
through grass that's one foot tall
that's the way the rattler goes
if you catch a glimpse at all.
I killed snakes once, about a score
in Africa and in Brazil
yet they filled me with such awe

it seemed gross sacrilege to kill.
Once with matchet and domestic broom
I duelled with a hooded snake
with frightened children in the room
and all our lives at stake.
The snake and I swayed to and fro.
I swung the broom. Her thick hood spread.
I jabbed the broom. She rode the blow
and I hacked off her hooded head.
Then I lopped this 'laithly worm'
and sliced the creature into nine
reptilian lengths that I saw squirm
as if still one connected spine.
The gaps between the bits I'd lopped
seemed supple snake though made of air
so that I wondered where life stopped
and if death started, where?
Since that time I've never killed
any snake that's come my way
between the wild land and the tilled
where I walk every day
towards my woodland writing shed,
my heart mysteriously stirred
if I get a glimpse of tail or head
or think its rattle's what I heard
when it's only a cicada's chirr
that grates on my cocked ear
not the hidden it/him/her
it so scares me to hear.
I've tried at last to come to terms
and deal only through my craft
with this laithliest of laithly worms
with poison fore, grim music aft
that makes my heart jam up my throat
and fills me with fear and wonder
as at the sound made when *Der Tod*
(in Strasbourg) *schlägt die Stunde*.
The sainted heroes of the Church

beheaded serpents who stood for
the Mother whose name they had to smirch
to get their own foot in the door.
We had to fight you to survive:
Darkness versus Light!
Now I want you on my land alive
and I don't want to fight.
Smitten by Jehovah's curses:
On thy belly thou must go!
I don't think Light is what you're versus
though the Bible tells me so.
I've seen you basking in the sun.
I've seen you entering the earth.
Darkness and Light to you are one.
You link together death and birth.
The Bible has another fable
that almost puts us on a par,
how God smote low ambitious Babel
for trying to reach too far.
From being once your mortal foe
and wanting all your kind to die
because the Bible told me so,
I now almost identify.
So, snake, old rhyming slang's
equivalent for looking glass,
when I walk here draw back your fangs
and let your unlikely ally pass.
I'm walking to my shed to write
and work out how they're linked
what's called the Darkness and the Light
before we all become extinct.
Laithly, maybe, but Earth-lover,
unmolested, let me go.
so my struggles might discover
what you already know.
As the low-flying fire-patrol
makes the slash and live-oaks sway
I go past the deep-dug gopher hole

where I hope my snake will stay
and stay forever if it likes.
I swear no one on this land will kill
the rattlesnake unless it strikes
then, I give my word, I will.
This fire-gap we trim with care
and mow short twice a year
is where we sometimes spot a hare,
a polecat, snake or deer.
They're off so fast one scarcely sees
retreating scut or tail
before they're lost among the trees
and they've thrown you off their trail.
But there's one who doesn't make
quick dashes for the undergrowth
nor bolts for the barley, that's the snake
whose length can bridge them both.
I've seen it span the fire-gap,
its whole six feet stretched out,
the wild touched by its rattle tip,
the tilled field by its snout.
Stretched out where the scrub's been mown
the rattler's lordly manner
treats the earth as all its own,
gap, cereals, savannah.
Best keep to my land if you're wise.
Once you cross my boundary line
the Bible-belters exorcize
all traces of the serpentine,
from Satan plain to demon drink
the flesh you're blamed for keeping hot,
all earth-embracing snakes that slink
whether poisonous or not,
the fairy, pacifist, the Red,
maybe somebody who loves the Muse
are all forms of the serpent's head
their God tells them to bruise,

e God invoked in Titusville
last night's local news
ainst the enemies they'd kill
ith the blessed and baptised Cruise.

I fear they're not the sort to see,
these Christians of the South,
the only real eternity
is a tale (like your tail) in the mouth.

Following Pine

I

When a plumber glues some lengths of PVC
that pipe our cold spring water from its source,
or a carpenter fits porch-posts, and they see,
from below or from above, the heartwood floors
made from virgin lumber, such men say,
as if they'd taught each other the same line:
Boards like them boards don't exist today!
then maybe add: *Now everything's new pine.*

Though the house is in a scant surviving wood
that has black walnut, hackberry, pecan
and moss-festooned live-oaks that have withstood
centuries more of bad news than a man,
sometimes we can drive an hour or more
and see nothing but dense pine trees on both sides
and no glimpse of the timbers for such floors
from virgin forest laid for virgin brides.

The feller/buncher and delimber groans,
grappling the grovelling pines, and dozing flat
a whole stand to a mess of stumps and stones
like some Goliath gorged on them, then shat
what was no use to him back on the land.
The sun and moon are sharing the same sky
as we drive by this totally depleted stand
marked down for GP planks and layer-peeled ply.

We'd set off early but shrill loggers' saws
were already shrieking in the stands of pines.
Fresh-felled, lopped slash pine tree-trunks in their scores
were being bull-dozed into ordered lines
waiting for the trucks in long convoy.
The trimmed-off branches were already burning.

The quiet, early road we'd wanted to enjoy
we did, but met the timber trucks returning.

Our early start was so that we could get
the trees we'd gone to buy into the ground,
watered and well-mulched, before sunset,
and not be digging in the dark with snakes around.
So with fig-trees, vines, and apples in the back,
wilting and losing their *Tree Garden* sheen,
we see on the road ahead a sky half black
and half as brilliantly blue as it had been.

The fast track was all wet, the crawler lane
we'd driven in most of the morning, dry.
The west side was in sun, the east in rain.
The east had black, the west had bright blue sky.
Armadillo blood, on the one side, 's washed away,
and, on the other, further on, sun-dried,
according as the car-crushed creature lay
on the highway's wet or sunny side.

Killed by traffic flowing through the night,
armadillos, rats, snake, dog, racoon,
dead on both road verges, left and right,
are scavenged on and half-decayed by noon,
and browsed over with hummed hubbub by blowfly
like loud necklaces, beads gone berserk,
that, whatever the day's weather, wet or dry,
stay a high gloss green and do their work.

And as we accelerated fast and overtook,
moving on the rain side as we did,
first one and then another timber truck,
the sudden wet road made me scared we'd skid.
My heart leaped instantly into my mouth
till we seemed safe between two loads of pine,
part of that convoy travelling due South
with east lane raining, and west side fine.

Was it the danger that made me hold my breath,
the quick injection of adrenalin,
the vision of our simultaneous death
and the crushed Toyota we were riding in,
or the giant raindrops that were pelting
onto the windshield and shot through with sun,
that made it seem the two of us were melting
and in a radiant decay becoming one?

Good job with such visions going on
that you were driving and you kept your head,
or that sense of fleshly glory would be gone
with the visionary who sensed it, and you, dead,
as dead as the armadillo, possum or racoon
killed by the nighttime traffic and well
advanced into decay by afternoon
and already giving off a putrid smell.

At least the storm cleaned love-bugs off the car
and washed the windscreen glass so you could drive.
When they copulate in swarms you can't see far.
They'd sooner fuck their brains out than survive.
They hit the car, embracing, and, squashed flat,
their twinned remains are merged into one mess.
Is it just the crushed canoodling gnat
that needs for its Nirvana nothingness?

Flattened in airborne couples as they fucked
their squashed millions would make the windscreen dark
if the wipers didn't constantly conduct
the dead to sectors round the dozed-clear arc.
Choked radiators, speckled bumper bars
splattered with love-bugs, two by two,
camouflage the colour of parked cars
pulled up at *Chiang's Mongolian Barbecue*.

From then on we were well and truly stuck
and anxious to get back to plant our trees
behind the huge pine-loaded lumber truck,
its red flag flapping in its slipstream breeze.

Because the lashed lopped slash was newly cut
the pungency of pine filled all the air.
We have to drive with all the windows shut,
the smell of pine too powerful to bear.

Now quite impossible to overtake
the convoy crawls up Highway 26.
Your foot keeps hovering above the brake
behind future coffin lids and cocktail sticks.
Our impatience at the slowness of the road
was not repugnance at the smell of pine,
however pungent, but worry for our load
of apple, pear, and fig, and muscadine.

Pine's the lingering perfume newly-weds
in just-built houses smell off panelling,
off squeaky floorboards, off their platform beds,
that cows smell when their rheumy nostrils sting
and tingle on electric pasture fences,
of the USA's best-selling bathroom spray
spritzed against those stinks that shock the senses,
shit, decomposition, and decay.

This is the smell in Walden that Thoreau's
cabin-builder's hands gave to his lunch,
the resinous pitch that prickled in his nose
whenever he took a sandwich out to munch,
and, maybe, thinking morosely as he chews
how woodlands mostly end up wooden goods,
the wrapping of his butties, week-old news,
was also nature once, and someone's woods.

In some sub-Walden worlds his dream survives
though these dreams of independence are nightmares
where retiree DIYers save their lives
while everyone around them 's losing theirs.
Spacemen go one way, these pioneers
mole down into the earth to find a place
to weather out the days, weeks, even years
that may well, but for these, kill off our race.

Considering their years it's maybe kinder
when they burrow in the ground like gophers do
not to offer them the sobering reminder
that rattlesnakes use gopher burrows too.
However layered with rocks and earth the roof,
however stocked with freeze-drieds (praise the Lord!)
however broad the door, how bullet proof,
no matter how much water they have stored,

until the radiation count all-clear
broadcast (they don't say how) on radio,
when they can, but cautiously, then reappear,
death got there before them, though they grow
by battery-powered Mazda lightbulb beams
alfalfa sprouts, damp blotting pads of cress,
while nations torn apart by common dreams
are united in a state of Nothingness.

Being neither newly-weds nor retirees
today we bought five figs, a pear, a vine,
and still have some belief in planting trees
with lifespans more than three times yours and mine.
Most of my life I've wanted to believe
those words of Luther that I've half-endorsed
about planting an apple tree the very eve
of the Apocalypse; or the Holocaust.

Every time my bags of red goat leather
are lying labelled England in the hall
and we take our last stroll round the land together
whether it's winter, summer, spring or fall,
there's always one last job I find to do,
pruned branches that I need to burn,
one last load of needles left to strew –
it's a way of guaranteeing my return.

A neighbour learns the skills they call 'survival'
living wild off sabal palm and game
killed by various means, knife, bow, or rifle,
even by throttling; me, I've learned to name

and know the subtle differences between
what once was only 'woods', or was before
mere nameless leaves of slightly varied green
but is now, say, persimmon or possumhaw.

Who lives for the future, who for now?
What good's the *cigale*'s way or the *fourmi*'s
if both end up as nothing anyhow
unless they look at life like Socrates
who wished, at the very end, to learn to play
a new air on his novice lyre. *Why?*
said his teacher, *this is your last day*.
To know it before I die, was the reply.

II

Chill, sterile, waterless, inert,
but full, the moon illuminates the night
enough for us to dig the still warm dirt
and plant the trees we've brought home by its light.
That globe above so different from here,
where no one lives and nothing ever grows,
no soil, no moisture and no atmosphere
to culture kumquats in or grow a rose.

From that great plain of death, inert and chill,
light may rebound but life will never come.
Those so-called seas are sterile, dry and still,
Mare Serenitatis, Sinus Iridum.
And yet, I thought, and yet, where would we be
without these light beams bounced off that dead land,
without these ungrassed dunes and lifeless sea
shedding their pallor on my scooping hand?

Light from a surface so cold and so dead
was the one we planted our new fruit-trees by,
the one that casts its glow now on our bed,
the one I find reflected in your eye.
Is not extinction with its eerie light
the appropriate presider when one swears
to sustain each other through the world of night
we've both decided is 'best born in pairs'?

We see all that we need to by a light
beamed off a barrenness of pits and plain,
off the '69 Apollo landing site
where planted flag and giant step remain.
That place, some men aspire to, discovers,
with light reflected from plains pocked with pits,
plantlife, a yellow house, a pair of lovers,
uniting in their love deep opposites.

This Earth, and this Earth's sterile satellite
won't always be, like life and death, apart,
if Man's destructive mind with Nature's might

leaves the planet pitted lunar chart
with no one here to name its barren craters
after rainbows, or discoverers, or peace,
though there'll be peace when Earth's worst agitators
find in final dissolution their release.

Despite barricaded bolt-holes deep below
it's often said that what will come off best
once, step by step, we've reached All-Systems-Go,
of all life on this Earth, 's the lowliest:
these bugs tonight like high-roast coffee beans
that fling themselves at flames and self-destruct,
that blue wasp juicing bugs like tangerines,
fat bucking locusts jockeyed on and sucked,

these trawling spiders that have rigged their nets
halfway between our porchlamps and the night,
their dawn webs threaded with dew jewelettes
and hauls of flies caught lurching for our light.
A blundering beetle with black lacquered back
that dialled its liquidation to the spider's limb,
embalmed in abseil/bell-pull, a stored snack
swathed in white cerements of sticky scrim.

Phoning that zero gets the spider quick.
Each leg's in touch with 45 degrees
of laddered circle where the insects stick
on tacky wires their weaver walks with ease.
Even the love-bugs, randy and ridiculous,
coupling regardless of death close behind
could still be fucking after all of us
are merged in the molten mess made of Mankind.

Falling asleep to loud cicada chirrs,
to scuttling cockroach, crashing carapace,
the noises that I hear are our inheritors
who'll know the Earth both B. and A. our race.
And underneath those floorboards of good heart
I think I hear the slither of a snake
and then the rodent prey the snake makes start.
Let's forget about the world until we wake!

III

Each board of 'tongue in groove' 's scored by a line
I measure insect movements by from bed.
A spider crossing long since scentless pine
racks its nightcatch on a slender thread.
The blowfly's hawsered body still looks wet
though all night it's been suspended in the dry.
It spins round, flashing, in the spider's net
with shredded cockroach wings and antennae.

I knew I'd wake today and find you gone
and look out of the window, knowing where
you'd be so early, still with nothing on,
watering our new plants with drowsy care.
The night, already stripped of half its dark,
now with the rest sloughed off, 's revealed as day,
and the sun already makes small rainbows arc
out of the hose's nozzle drizzling spray.

Crunching the rusted needles that I strew
to stunt the weed growth on the paths we hacked
I come towards you and am naked too,
and, being naked, feel my nerves react
to the pliant give and snap of spider thread,
snagged on a nipple, sliding on my sweat,
pinged on a whisker, snapped against my head –
the night survivor loosened from the net.

Though impossible to hear I sense each ping
as of an instrument too tautly strung
with notes too high for human voice to sing
and, in any case, not heard if ever sung,
and maybe like that air of Socrates,
I hope he played at least once with some skill,
transposed beyond our ken into high keys
I can't hear now, and know I never will.

For all that unseen threads break on my face,
for all these cordons of cobweb caress

I walk towards you and don't change my pace
feeling each broken thread one stricture less
against my passage to the world of day.
I can only know the last one when it breaks.
You can't see them ahead, and anyway,
I have to scan the ground for rattlesnakes.

I wonder as I walk still half awake
if the trees that baked a bit long in the boot
and we'd planted in the dark would ever take
and if we'd ever taste their hoped-for fruit.
I pass what's become in 12 months gut-high pine
planted last summer in a long close row
as our few acres' demarcation line
and I will what's still a hedge to grow less slow,

and be tall enough to mask the present view
of you watering the saplings as you spray
rainbows at fig-trees planted 2-1-2
and both of us still nude at break of day.
A morning incense smokes off well-doused ground.
Everywhere you water rainbows shine.
This private haven that we two have found
might be the more so when enclosed with pine.

Cypress & Cedar

A smell comes off my pencil as I write
in the margins of a sacred Sanskrit text.
By just sufficient candlelight I skim
these scriptures sceptically from hymn to hymn.
The bits I read aloud to you I've Xed
for the little clues they offer to life's light.

I sit in mine, and you sit in your chair.
A sweetness hangs round yours; a foul smell mine.
Though the house still has no windows and no doors
and the tin roof's roughly propped with 4 × 4s
that any gale could jolt, our chairs are fine
and both scents battle for the same night air.

Near Chiefland just off US 129,
from the clapboard abattoir about a mile,
the local sawyer Bob displays his wares:
porch swings, picnic tables, lounging chairs,
rough sawn and nailed together 'cracker' style.
The hand I shake leaves powerful smells on mine.

Beside two piles of shavings, white and red,
one fragrant as a perfume, and one rank
and malodorous from its swampland ooze,
Bob displayed that week's work's chairs for me to choose.
I chose one that was sweet, and one that stank,
and thought about the sweet wood for a bed.

To quote the carpenter he 'stinks o' shite'
and his wife won't sleep with him on cypress days,
but after a day of cedar, so he said,
she comes back eagerly into his bed,
and, as long as he works cedar, there she stays.
Sometimes he scorns the red wood and works white!

Today I've laboured with my hands for hours
sawing fenceposts up for winter; one tough knot
jolted the chainsaw at my face and sprayed
a beetroot cedar dust off the bucked blade,
along with damp earth with its smell of rot,
hurtling beetles, termites in shocked showers.

To get one gatepost free I had to tug
for half an hour, but dragged up from its hole
it smelled, down even to the last four feet
rammed in the ground, still beautifully sweet
as if the grave had given life parole
and left the sour earth perfumed where I'd dug.

Bob gave me a cedar buckle for my belt,
and after the whole day cutting, stacking wood,
damp denim, genitals, 'genuine hide leather'
all these fragrances were bound together
by cedar, and together they smelled good.
It was wonderful the way my trousers smelled.

I can't help but suppose flesh-famished Phèdre
would have swept that prissy, epicene,
big-game hunting stepson Hippolyte,
led by his nose to cedar, off his feet,
and left no play at all for poor Racine,
if she'd soaped her breasts with *Bois de Cèdre*.

If in doubt ask Bob the sawyer's wife!
Pet lovers who can't stand the stink of cat
buy sacks of litter that's been 'cedarized'
and from ancient times the odour's been much prized.
Though not a Pharaoh I too favour that
for freighting my rank remains out of this life.

Why not two cedar chairs? Why go and buy
a reeking cypress chair as a reminder,
as if one's needed, of primeval ooze,
like swamps near Suwannee backroads, or bayous,
stagnation Mother Nature left behind her
hauling Mankind up from mononuclei?

Cypress still has roots in that old stew
paddling its origins in protozoa,
the stew where consciousness that writes and reads
grew its first squat tail from slimy seeds.
I'd've used it for the Ark if I'd been Noah,
though cedar, I know you'll say, would also do.

This place not in the *Blue Guide* or in *Fodor*
between the Suwannee River and the Styx
named by some homesick English classicist
who loved such puns, loathed swamps, and, lonely, pissed
his livelihood away with redneck hicks
and never once enjoyed the cedar's odour,

or put its smoke to snake-deterrent use
prescribed by Virgil in his *Georgics* III
with *chelydrus* here in the US South
construed as the diamondback or cottonmouth
which freed him, some said, from his misery.
Others said liquor, and others still a noose.

And, evenings, he, who'd been an avid reader
of the *Odyssey* and *Iliad* in Greek,
became an even avider verandah drinker
believing sourmash made a Stoic thinker
though stuck with no paddle up Phlegethon's creek,
and had no wife with clothes chest of sweet cedar.

But you bought one at Bob's place and you keep
your cotton frocks in it, your underwear,
and such a fragrance comes from your doffed bras
as come from uncorked phials in hot bazaars,
and when you take your clothes off and lie bare
your body breathes out cedar while you sleep.

That lonely English exile named the river,
though it could have been someone like me, for whom,
though most evenings on the porch I read and write,
there's often such uneasiness in night
it creates despair in me, or drinker's gloom
that could send later twinges through the liver.

Tonight so far 's been peaceful with no lightning.
The pecan trees and hophornbeams are still.
The storm's held off, the candleflame's quite straight,
the fire and wick united in one fate.
Though this quietness that can, one moment, fill
the heart with peace, can, the next, be frightening –

A hog gets gelded with a gruesome squeal
that skids across the quietness of night
to where we're sitting on our dodgy porch.
I reach for Seth Tooke's shotgun and the torch
then realize its 'farmwork' so alright
but my flesh also flinches from the steel.

Peace like a lily pad on swamps of pain –
floating's its only way of being linked.
This consciousness of ours that reads and writes
drifts on a darkness deeper than the night's.
Above that blackness, buoyed on the extinct,
peace, pure-white, floats flowering in the brain,

and fades, as finally the nenuphar
we found on a pewter swamp where two roads ended
was also bound to fade. The head and heart
are neither of them too much good apart
and peace comes in the moments that they're blended
as cypress and cedar at this moment are.

My love, as prone as I am to despair,
I think the world of night's best born in pairs,
one half we'll call the female, one the male,
though neither essence need, in love, prevail.
We sit here in distinctly scented chairs
you, love, in the cedar, me the cypress chair.

Though tomorrow night I might well sit in yours
and you in mine, the blended scent's the same
since I pushed my chair close to your chair
and we read by the one calm candle that we share
in this wilderness that might take years to tame,
this house still with no windows and no doors.

Let the candle cliché come out of the chill –
'the flickering candle on a vast dark plain'
of one lone voice against the state machine,
or Mimi's on cold stairs aren't what I mean
but moments like this now when heart and brain
seem one sole flame that's bright and straight and still.

If it's in Levy County that I die
(though fearing I'd feel homesick as I died
I'd sooner croak in Yorkshire if I could)
I'll have my coffin made of cedar wood
to balance the smell like cypress from inside
and hope the smoke of both blends in the sky,

as both scents from our porch chairs do tonight.
'Tvashti', says this Indian Rig Veda,
'hewed the world out of one tree,' but doesn't tell,
since for durability both do as well,
if the world he made was cypress wood; or cedar
the smell coming off my pencil as I write.

v.

'My father still reads the dictionary every day. He says your life depends on your power to master words.'

Arthur Scargill, *Sunday Times*, 10 Jan. 1982

Next millennium you'll have to search quite hard
to find my slab behind the family dead,
butcher, publican, and baker, now me, bard
adding poetry to their beef, beer and bread.

With Byron three graves on I'll not go short
of company, and Wordsworth's opposite.
That's two peers already, of a sort,
and we'll all be thrown together if the pit,

whose galleries once ran beneath this plot,
causes the distinguished dead to drop
into the rabblement of bone and rot,
shored slack, crushed shale, smashed prop.

Wordsworth built church organs, Byron tanned
luggage cowhide in the age of steam,
and knew their place of rest before the land
caves in on the lowest worked-out seam.

This graveyard on the brink of Beeston Hill's
the place I may well rest if there's a spot
under the rose roots and the daffodils
by which dad dignified the family plot.

If buried ashes saw then I'd survey
the places I learned Latin, and learned Greek,
and left, the ground where Leeds United play
but disappoint their fans week after week,

which makes them lose their sense of self-esteem
and taking a short cut home through these graves here
they reassert the glory of their team
by spraying words on tombstones, pissed on beer.

This graveyard stands above a worked-out pit.
Subsidence makes the obelisks all list.
One leaning left's marked FUCK, one right's marked
  SHIT
sprayed by some peeved supporter who was pissed.

Far-sighted for his family's future dead,
but for his wife, this banker's still alone
on his long obelisk, and doomed to head
a blackened dynasty of unclaimed stone,

now graffitied with a crude four-letter word.
His children and grand-children went away
and never came back home to be interred,
so left a lot of space for skins to spray.

The language of this graveyard ranges from
a bit of Latin for a former Mayor
or those who laid their lives down at the Somme,
the hymnal fragments and the gilded prayer,

how people 'fell asleep in the Good Lord',
brief chisellable bits from the good book
and rhymes whatever length they could afford,
to CUNT, PISS, SHIT and (mostly) FUCK!

Or, more expansively, there's LEEDS v.
the opponent of last week, this week, or next,
and a repertoire of blunt four-letter curses
on the team or race that makes the sprayer vexed.

Then, pushed for time, or fleeing some observer,
dodging between tall family vaults and trees
like his team's best ever winger, dribbler, swerver,
fills every space he finds with versus Vs.

Vs sprayed on the run at such a lick,
the sprayer master of his flourished tool,
get short-armed on the left like that red tick
they never marked his work much with at school.

Half this skinhead's age but with approval
I helped whitewash a V on a brick wall.
No one clamoured in the press for its removal
or thought the sign, in wartime, rude at all.

These Vs are all the versuses of life
from LEEDS v. DERBY, Black/White
and (as I've known to my cost) man v. wife,
Communist v. Fascist, Left v. Right,

class v. class as bitter as before,
the unending violence of US and THEM,
personified in 1984
by Coal Board MacGregor and the NUM,

Hindu/Sikh, soul/body, heart v. mind,
East/West, male/female, and the ground
these fixtures are fought out on 's Man, resigned
to hope from his future what his past never found.

The prospects for the present aren't too grand
when a swastika with NF (National Front) 's
sprayed on a grave, to which another hand
has added, in a reddish colour, CUNTS.

Which is, I grant, the word that springs to mind,
when going to clear the weeds and rubbish thrown
on the family plot by football fans, I find
UNITED graffitied on my parents' stone.

How many British graveyards now this May
are strewn with rubbish and choked up with weeds
since families and friends have gone away
for work or fuller lives, like me from Leeds?

When I first came here 40 years ago
with my dad to 'see my grandma' I was 7.
I helped dad with the flowers. He let me know
she'd gone to join my grandad up in Heaven.

My dad who came each week to bring fresh flowers
came home with clay stains on his trouser knees.
Since my parents' deaths I've spent 2 hours
made up of odd 10 minutes such as these.

Flying visits once or twice a year,
and though I'm horrified just who's to blame
that I find instead of flowers cans of beer
and more than one grave sprayed with some skin's name?

Where there were flower urns and troughs of water
and mesh receptacles for withered flowers
are the HARP tins of some skinhead Leeds supporter.
It isn't all his fault though. Much is ours.

5 kids, with one in goal, play 2-a-side.
When the ball bangs on the hawthorn that's one post
and petals fall they hum *Here Comes the Bride*
though not so loud they'd want to rouse a ghost.

They boot the ball on purpose at the trunk
and make the tree shed showers of shrivelled may.
I look at this word graffitied by some drunk
and I'm in half a mind to let it stay.

(Though honesty demands that I say *if*
I'd wanted to take the necessary pains
to scrub the skin's inscription off
I only had an hour between trains.

So the feelings that I had as I stood gazing
and the significance I saw could be a sham,
mere excuses for not patiently erasing
the word sprayed on the grave of dad and mam.)

This pen's all I have of magic wand.
I know this world's so torn but want no other
except for dad who'd hoped from 'the beyond'
a better life than this one, *with* my mother.

Though I don't believe in afterlife at all
and know it's cheating it's hard *not* to make
a sort of furtive prayer from this skin's scrawl,
his UNITED mean 'in Heaven' for their sake,

an accident of meaning to redeem
an act intended as mere desecration
and make the thoughtless spraying of his team
apply to higher things, and to the nation.

Some, where kids use aerosols, use giant signs
to let the people know who's forged their fetters
like PRI CE O WALES above West Yorkshire mines
(no prizes for who nicked the missing letters!)

The big blue star for booze, tobacco ads,
the magnet's monogram, the royal crest,
insignia in neon dwarf the lads
who spray a few odd FUCKS when they're depressed.

Letters of transparent tubes and gas
in Düsseldorf are blue and flash out KRUPP.
Arms are hoisted for the British ruling class
and clandestine, genteel aggro keeps them up.

And there's HARRISON on some Leeds building site,
I've taken in fun as blazoning my name,
which I've also seen on books, in Broadway lights,
so why can't skins with spraycans do the same?

But why inscribe these *graves* with CUNT and SHIT?
Why choose neglected tombstones to disfigure?
This pitman's of last century daubed PAKI GIT,
this grocer Broadbent's aerosolled with NIGGER?

They're there to shock the living not arouse
the dead from their deep peace to lend support
for the causes skinhead spraycans could espouse.
The dead would want their desecrators caught!

Jobless though they are how can these kids,
even though their team's lost one more game,
believe that the 'Pakis', 'Niggers', even 'Yids'
sprayed on the tombstones here should bear the blame?

What is it that these crude words are revealing?
What is it that this aggro act implies?
Giving the dead their xenophobic feeling
or just a *cri-de-coeur* because man dies?

So what's a cri-de-coeur, *cunt? Can't you speak*
the language that yer mam spoke. Think of 'er!
Can yer only get yer tongue round fucking Greek?
Go and fuck yerself with cri-de-coeur!

'She didn't talk like you do for a start!'
I shouted, turning where I thought the voice had been.
She didn't understand yer fucking 'art'!
She thought yer fucking poetry obscene!

I wish on this skin's word deep aspirations,
first the prayer for my parents I can't make
then a call to Britain and to all the nations
made in the name of love for peace's sake.

Aspirations, cunt! Folk on t'fucking dole
'ave got about as much scope to aspire
above the shit they're dumped in, cunt, as coal
aspires to be chucked on t'fucking fire.

OK, forget the aspirations. Look, I know
United's losing gets you fans incensed
and how far the HARP inside you makes you go
but *all* these Vs: against! against! against!

Ah'll tell yer then what really riles a bloke.
It's reading on their graves the jobs they did –
butcher, publican and baker. Me, I'll croak
doing t'same nowt ah do now as a kid.

'ard birth ah wor, mi mam says, almost killed 'er.
Death after life on t'dole won't seem as 'ard!
Look at this cunt, Wordsworth, organ builder,
this fucking 'aberdasher Appleyard!

If mi mam's up there, don't want to meet 'er
listening to me list mi dirty deeds,
and 'ave to pipe up to St fucking Peter
ah've been on t'dole all mi life in fucking Leeds!

Then t' Alleluias stick in t' angels' gobs.
When dole-wallahs fuck off to the void
what'll t'mason carve up for their jobs?
The cunts who lieth 'ere wor unemployed?

This lot worked at one job all life through.
Byron, 'Tanner', 'Lieth 'ere interred'
They'll chisel fucking poet when they do you
and that, yer cunt, 's a crude four-letter word.

'Listen, cunt!' I said, 'before you start your jeering
the reason why I want this in a book
's to give ungrateful cunts like you a hearing!'
A book, yer stupid cunt, 's not worth a fuck!

'The only reason why I write this poem at all
on yobs like you who do the dirt on death
's to give some higher meaning to your scrawl.'
Don't fucking bother, cunt! Don't waste your breath!

'You piss-artist skinhead cunt, you wouldn't know
and it doesn't fucking matter if you do,
the skin and poet united fucking Rimbaud
but the autre that je est is fucking you.'

Ah've told yer, no more Greek . . . That's yer last warning.
Ah'll boot yer fucking balls to Kingdom Come.
They'll find yer cold on t'grave tomorrer morning.
So don't speak Greek. Don't treat me like I'm dumb.

'I've done my bits of mindless aggro too
not half a mile from where we're standing now.'
Yeah, ah bet yer wrote a poem, yer wanker you!
'No, shut yer gob a while. Ah'll tell yer 'ow . . .

'Herman Darewski's band played operetta
with a wobbly soprano warbling. Just why
I made my mind up that I'd got to get her
with the fire hose I can't say, but I'll try.

It wasn't just the singing angered me.
At the same time half a crowd was jeering
as the smooth Hugh Gaitskell, our MP,
made promises the other half were cheering.

What I hated in those high soprano ranges
was uplift beyond all reason and control
and in a world where you say nothing changes
it seemed a sort of prick-tease of the soul.

I tell you when I heard high notes that rose
above Hugh Gaitskell's cool electioneering
straight from the warbling throat right up my nose
I had all your aggro in *my* jeering.

And I hit the fire extinguisher ON knob
and covered orchestra and audience with spray.
I could run as fast as you then. A good job!
They yelled "damned vandal" after me that day . . .'

And then yer saw the light and gave up 'eavy!
And knew a man's not how much he can sup . . .
Yer reward for growing up's this super-bevvy,
a meths and champagne punch in t' FA Cup.

Ah've 'eard all that from old farts past their prime.
'ow now yer live wi' all yer once detested . . .
Old farts with not much left 'll give me time.
Fuckers like that get folks like me arrested.

Covet not thy neighbour's wife, thy neighbour's riches.
Vicar and cop who say, to save our souls,
Get thee behind me, Satan, drop their *breeches*
and get the Devil's dick right up their 'oles!

It was more a working marriage that I'd meant,
a blend of masculine and feminine.
Ignoring me, he started looking, bent
on some more aerosolling, for his tin.

'It was more a working marriage that I mean!'
Fuck, and save mi soul, eh? That suits me.
Then as if I'd egged him on to be obscene
he added a middle slit to one daubed V.

Don't talk to me of fucking representing
the class yer were born into any more.
Yer going to get 'urt and start resenting
it's not poetry we need in this class war.

Yer've given yerself toffee, cunt. Who needs
yer fucking poufy words. Ah write mi own.
Ah've got mi work on show all over Leeds
like this UNITED 'ere on some sod's stone.

'OK!' (thinking I had him trapped) 'OK!'
'If you're so proud of it then sign your name
when next you're full of HARP and armed with spray,
next time you take this short cut from the game.'

He took the can, contemptuous, unhurried
and cleared the nozzle and prepared to sign
the UNITED sprayed where mam and dad were buried.
He aerosolled his name. And it was mine.

The boy footballers bawl *Here Comes the Bride*
and drifting blossoms fall onto my head.
One half of me 's alive but one half died
when the skin half sprayed my name among the dead.

Half versus half, the enemies within
the heart that can't be whole till they unite.
As I stoop to grab the crushed HARP lager tin
the day's already dusk, half dark, half light.

That UNITED that I'd wished onto the nation
or as reunion for dead parents soon recedes.
The word's once more a mindless desecration
by some HARPoholic yob supporting Leeds.

Almost the time for ghosts I'd better scram.
Though not given much to fears of spooky scaring
I don't fancy an encounter with my mam
playing Hamlet with me for this swearing.

Though I've a train to catch my step is slow.
I walk on the grass and graves with wary tread
over these subsidences, these shifts below
the life of Leeds supported by the dead.

Further underneath's that cavernous hollow
that makes the gravestones lean towards the town.
A matter of mere time and it will swallow
this place of rest and all the resters down.

I tell myself I've got, say, 30 years.
At 75 this place will suit me fine.
I've never feared the grave but what I fear's
that great worked-out black hollow under mine.

Not train departure time, and not Town Hall
with the great white clock face I can see,
coal, that began, with no man here at all,
as 300 million-year-old plant debris.

5 kids still play at making blossoms fall
and humming as they do *Here Comes the Bride*.
They never seem to tire of their ball
though I hear a woman's voice call one inside.

2 larking boys play bawdy bride and groom.
3 boys in Leeds strip la-la *Lohengrin*.
I hear them as I go through growing gloom
still years away from being skald or skin.

The ground's carpeted with petals as I throw
the aerosol, the HARP can, the cleared weeds
on top of dad's dead daffodils, then go,
with not one glance behind, away from Leeds.

The bus to the station's still the no. 1
but goes by routes that I don't recognize.
I look out for known landmarks as the sun
reddens the swabs of cloud in darkening skies.

Home, home, home, to my woman as the red
darkens from a fresh blood to a dried.
Home, home to my woman, home to bed
where opposites seem sometimes unified.

A pensioner in turban taps his stick
along the pavement past the corner shop,
that sells samosas now not beer on tick,
to the Kashmir Muslim Club that was the Co-op.

House after house FOR SALE where we'd played cricket
with white roses cut from flour-sacks on our caps,
with stumps chalked on the coal-grate for our wicket,
and every one bought now by 'coloured chaps',

dad's most liberal label as he felt
squeezed by the unfamiliar, and fear
of foreign food and faces, when he smelt
curry in the shop where he'd bought beer.

And growing frailer, 'wobbly on his pins'
the shops he felt familiar with withdrew
which meant much longer tiring treks for tins
that had a label on them that he knew.

And as the shops that stocked his favourites receded
whereas he'd fancied beans and popped next door,
he found that four long treks a week were needed
till he wondered what he bothered eating for.

The supermarket made him feel embarrassed.
Where people bought whole lambs for family freezers
he bought baked beans from check-out girls too harassed
to smile or swap a joke with sad old geezers.

But when he bought his cigs he'd have a chat,
his week's one conversation, truth to tell,
but time also came and put a stop to that
when old Wattsy got bought out by M. Patel.

And there, 'Time like an ever rolling stream' 's
what I once trilled behind that boarded front.
A 1,000 ages made coal-bearing seams
and even more the hand that sprayed this CUNT

on both Methodist and C of E billboards
once divided in their fight for local souls.
Whichever house more truly was the Lord's
both's pews are filled with cut-price toilet rolls.

Home, home to my woman, never to return
till sexton or survivor has to cram
the bits of clinker scooped out of my urn
down through the rose-roots to my dad and mam.

Home, home to my woman, where the fire's lit
these still chilly mid-May evenings, home to you,
and perished vegetation from the pit
escaping insubstantial up the flue.

Listening to *Lulu*, in our hearth we burn,
as we hear the high Cs rise in stereo,
what was lush swamp club-moss and tree-fern
at least 300 million years ago.

Shilbottle cobbles, Alban Berg high D
lifted from a source that bears your name,
the one we hear decay, the one we see,
the fern from the foetid forest, as brief flame.

This world, with far too many people in,
starts on the TV logo as a taw,
then ping-pong, tennis, football; then one spin
to show us all, then shots of the Gulf War.

As the coal with reddish dust cools in the grate
on the late-night national news we see
police v. pickets at a coke-plant gate,
old violence and old disunity.

The map that's colour-coded Ulster/Eire's
flashed on again as almost every night.
Behind a tiny coffin with two bearers
men in masks with arms show off their might.

The day's last images recede to first a glow
and then a ball that shrinks back to blank screen.
Turning to love, and sleep's oblivion, I know
what the UNITED that the skin sprayed *has* to mean.

Hanging my clothes up, from my parka hood
may and apple petals, browned and creased,
fall onto the carpet and bring back the flood
of feelings their first falling had released.

I hear like ghosts from all Leeds matches humming
with one concerted voice the bride, the bride
I feel united to, *my* bride is coming
into the bedroom, naked, to my side.

The ones we choose to love become our anchor
when the hawser of the blood-tie's hacked, or frays.
But a voice that scorns chorales is yelling: Wanker!
It's the aerosolling skin I met today's.

My *alter ego* wouldn't want to know it,
his aerosol vocab would baulk at LOVE,
the skin's UNITED underwrites the poet,
the measures carved below the ones above.

I doubt if 30 years of bleak Leeds·weather
and 30 falls of apple and of may
will erode the UNITED binding us together.
And now it's your decision: does it stay?

Next millennium you'll have to search quite hard
to find out where I'm buried but I'm near
the grave of haberdasher Appleyard,
the pile of HARPs, or some new neonned beer.

Find Byron, Wordsworth, or turn left between
one grave marked Broadbent, one marked Richardson.
Bring some solution with you that can clean
whatever new crude words have been sprayed on.

If love of art, or love, gives you affront
that the grave I'm in's graffitied then, maybe,
erase the more offensive FUCK and CUNT
but leave, with the worn UNITED, one small v.

victory? For vast, slow, coal-creating forces
that hew the body's seams to get the soul.
Will Earth run out of her 'diurnal courses'
before repeating her creation of black coal?

But choose a day like I chose in mid-May
or earlier when apple and hawthorn tree,
no matter if boys boot their ball all day,
cling to their blossoms and won't shake them free.

If, having come this far, somebody reads
these verses, and he/she wants to understand,
face this grave on Beeston Hill, your back to Leeds,
and read the chiselled epitaph I've planned:

Beneath your feet's a poet, then a pit.
Poetry supporter, if you're here to find
how poems can grow from (beat you to it!) SHIT
find the beef, the beer, the bread, then look behind.

FOR THE BEST IN PAPERBACKS, LOOK FOR THE ⬤

In every corner of the world, on every subject under the sun, Penguin represents quality and variety – the very best in publishing today.

For complete information about books available from Penguin – including Pelicans, Puffins, Peregrines and Penguin Classics – and how to order them, write to us at the appropriate address below. Please note that for copyright reasons the selection of books varies from country to country.

In the United Kingdom: Please write to *Dept E.P., Penguin Books Ltd, Harmondsworth, Middlesex, UB7 0DA*

If you have any difficulty in obtaining a title, please send your order with the correct money, plus ten per cent for postage and packaging, to *PO Box No 11, West Drayton, Middlesex*

In the United States: Please write to *Dept BA, Penguin, 299 Murray Hill Parkway, East Rutherford, New Jersey 07073*

In Canada: Please write to *Penguin Books Canada Ltd, 2801 John Street, Markham, Ontario L3R 1B4*

In Australia: Please write to the *Marketing Department, Penguin Books Australia Ltd, P.O. Box 257, Ringwood, Victoria 3134*

In New Zealand: Please write to the *Marketing Department, Penguin Books (NZ) Ltd, Private Bag, Takapuna, Auckland 9*

In India: Please write to *Penguin Overseas Ltd, 706 Eros Apartments, 56 Nehru Place, New Delhi, 110019*

In Holland: Please write to *Penguin Books Nederland B.V., Postbus 195, NL–1380AD Weesp, Netherlands*

In Germany: Please write to *Penguin Books Ltd, Friedrichstrasse 10–12, D–6000 Frankfurt Main 1, Federal Republic of Germany*

In Spain: Please write to *Longman Penguin España, Calle San Nicolas 15, E–28013 Madrid, Spain*

In France: Please write to *Penguin Books Ltd, 39 Rue de Montmorency, F-75003, Paris, France*

In Japan: Please write to *Longman Penguin Japan Co Ltd, Yamaguchi Building, 2–12–9 Kanda Jimbocho, Chiyoda-Ku, Tokyo 101, Japan*

Anna Akhmatova   Translated by D. M. Thomas

Anna Akhmatova is not only Russia's finest woman poet but perhaps the finest in the history of Western Culture.

Fernando Pessoa

'I have sought for his shade in those Edwardian cafés in Lisbon which he haunted, for he was Lisbon's Cavafy or Verlaine' – Cyril Connolly in the *Sunday Times*

Yehuda Amichai   Translated by Chana Bloch and Stephen Mitchell

'A truly major poet . . . there's a depth, breadth and weighty momentum in these subtle and delicate poems of his' – Ted Hughes

Czeslaw Milosz

Czeslaw Milosz received the Nobel Prize for Literature in 1980. 'One of the greatest poets of our time, perhaps the greatest' – Joseph Brodsky

To Urania   Joseph Brodsky
Winner of the 1987 Nobel Prize for Literature

Exiled from the Soviet Union in 1972, Joseph Brodsky has been universally acclaimed as the most talented Russian poet of his generation.

Philippe Jaccottet

This volume, contains the first translations into English of the poetry of Philippe Jaccottet, 'one of the finest European poets of the century'.

Osip Mandelstam   Translated by Clarence Brown and W. S. Merwin

Like his friends Pasternak and Akhmatova, Mandelstam, through his work, bore witness to the plight of Russia under Stalin – for which he paid with his life.

Pablo Neruda

From the poet-explorer of his early years to the poet-historian of 'my thin country', Neruda's personal turning point came when he was posted to Barcelona as Chilean consul just before the Spanish Civil War.

FOR THE BEST IN PAPERBACKS, LOOK FOR THE

A CHOICE OF PENGUINS AND PELICANS

The Literature of the United States   Marcus Cunliffe

The fourth edition of a masterly one-volume survey, described by D. W. Brogan in the *Guardian* as 'a very good book indeed'.

The Sceptical Feminist   Janet Radcliffe Richards

A rigorously argued but sympathetic consideration of feminist claims. 'A triumph' – *Sunday Times*

The Enlightenment   Norman Hampson

A classic survey of the age of Diderot and Voltaire, Goethe and Hume, which forms part of the Pelican History of European Thought.

Defoe to the Victorians   David Skilton

'Learned and stimulating' (*The Times Educational Supplement*). A fascinating survey of two centuries of the English novel.

Reformation to Industrial Revolution   Christopher Hill

This 'formidable little book' (Peter Laslett in the *Guardian*) by one of our leading historians is Volume 2 of the Pelican Economic History of Britain.

The New Pelican Guide to English Literature   Boris Ford (ed.)
Volume 8: The Present

This book brings a major series up to date with important essays on Ted Hughes and Nadine Gordimer, Philip Larkin and V. S. Naipaul, and all the other leading writers of today.

FOR THE BEST IN PAPERBACKS, LOOK FOR THE

PENGUIN BOOKS OF POETRY

American Verse
Ballads
British Poetry Since 1945
Caribbean Verse
A Choice of Comic and Curious Verse
Contemporary American Poetry
Contemporary British Poetry
Eighteenth-Century Verse
Elizabethan Verse
English Poetry 1918–60
English Romantic Verse
English Verse
First World War Poetry
Georgian Poetry
Irish Verse
Light Verse
London in Verse
Love Poetry
The Metaphysical Poets
Modern African Poetry
Modern Arab Poetry
New Poetry
Poems of Science
Poetry of the Thirties
Post-War Russian Poetry
Spanish Civil War Verse
Unrespectable Verse
Urdu Poetry
Victorian Verse
Women Poets